To Jacque Walker! God Bless You

WISE WOMEN PRAY

Keep Praying!

Rev. Adriane Blair Wise

WISE WOMEN PRAY

31 Days of Prayers to Fortify Your Faith

ADRIANE BLAIR WISE

WISE WOMEN PRAY: 31 Days of Prayers to Fortify Your Faith

Cover Design: Tina Long, Glenn Dale, Maryland

Photograph by: Valerie Woody, Valerie Woody Photography

Presented to

Occasion

Wise Women Pray is dedicated to My Lord and Savior, Jesus Christ, and to two very special women who taught me the power of prayer:

My beloved mother,

Gladys A. Blair

and my late maternal grandmother,

Mrs. Larau Young.

Wise Women Pray!

... when I call to remembrance the genuine faith that is in you, which dwelt first in your grandmother Lois and your mother Eunice, and I am persuaded is in you also. – 2 Timothy 1:5

CONTENTS

ACKNOWLEDGMENT

God, in His divine wisdom, receives all the glory for this book of prayers. I am forever grateful to God for allowing me to spend precious time in His presence, and I am humbled by His demonstration of extravagant love for me.

There are so many people who have contributed in tangible ways to my life and this book. I especially cherish the friends and family whose words of encouragement served as nourishment for the completion of this book.

I desire to express special appreciation to the Metropolitan Baptist Church and to my Pastor, Dr. Maurice Watson along with Mrs. Janice Watson for their continued prayers, support, and love as I live out God's call on my life.

I especially want to say a personal note of thanks to the members of the Women's Bible Study; your prayers of intercession, words of affirmation, and

financial support are appreciated more than you will ever know. You each are precious in my eyes, and I love you dearly.

To all the remarkable women and men who have ever attended a class that I have taught at MBC. My life is forever changed for the better because you have been a part of it.

To my father in ministry, Dr. H. Beecher Hicks, Jr., gratitude fills my heart for you writing the Foreword to this book. You and your lovely wife, Dr. Elizabeth Harrison Hicks have poured into my life for nearly twenty-seven years and I am forever inclined to say "thank you and much obliged" for claiming me as one of your own.

To my colleagues in ministry, Dr. Jesse Wood, Executive Pastor; Dr. Sherrill McMillan, Minister for Counseling and Family Services; Reverend Brenda Girton-Mitchell, Minister of Stewardship and Missions; and Reverend Nathaniel Yates Sr., Youth and Young Adults Pastor, I appreciate each of you and count it a privilege to serve in ministry with you.

A special note of thanks is extended to Reverend Brenda for challenging me to take my own advice and "get out of my own way." You know how I feel about you; your friendship and love are so very much appreciated.

To Reverend Melvin Milton Maxwell, my brother from another mother, and his beloved bride, my sister/girlfriend, Lady Cherry Maxwell, thank you for being my friends! Everyone should have friends like you! Your dedication and support never go unnoticed. I love you both to the moon and back for cheering me on to do the work God has purposed specifically for me.

To Dr. Cheryl Price, my big sister, thank you for your words of wisdom, knowledge, and understanding during this entire process. You have always been such an encouragement to me over the years; even from the early days of inviting me to teach your Bible Study class (your sneaky way of helping me to push past my fear of teaching the Word of God).

To Dr. Bernard Richardson, Dean of the Chapel at the Andrew Rankin Memorial Chapel, Howard University, thank you for the opportunity to serve as

the Baptist Chaplain for eight years on that campus. I also appreciate your constant support and conversations. The experience was priceless.

To the late Dr. Evans E. Crawford, Jr., for always being so supportive of my ministry and for these words, "One never knows what will come of it" as you encouraged me to put pen to paper and write down my prayers.

To Dr. Jeffrey Haggray, Executive Director of the American Baptist Home Mission, thank you for serving as my first pastor and mentor in ministry. Your words of affirmation and prophetic utterance about the call on my life and even this season of writing is forever appreciated. I am grateful to call you, Shelby, and the children my family.

To Pastor Mark Batterson, thank you for taking time to speak with me during your book signing and for these words of affirmation concerning writing my book, "Treat the nudging to write a book as *holy and a prayer within itself.*"

To the members of Alpha Kappa Alpha Sorority, Incorporate, especially those whom I have had the privilege of serving as your chapter chaplain, Rho Mu Omega; thank you for your sisterhood and friendship. Nearly twenty-five years ago, you gave

me a platform to practice ministry when you created a chaplain position and entrusted me with the assignment of fulfilling the accompanying duties.

To Soror Shari L. McCoy, former Basileus of Rho Mu Omega, thank you for the initial opportunity to serve as the first chapter Chaplain. I love you Boo!

To Soror Mary Bentley-LaMar, 34th North Atlantic Regional Director, thank you for the new appointment to serve as the Regional Chaplain for the North Atlantic Region.

To Soror Meredith Henderson, 33rd North Atlantic Regional Director, thank you for the appointment to serve as the Regional Prayer Team Co-Chairman along with Soror Denise Parker Lawrence.

To Soror Constance Pizarro, 32nd North Atlantic Regional Director, thank you for establishing the Prayer Team and for the appointment to serve as the Cluster 1 Prayer Team Leader.

To Soror Pamela Bates Porch, the International Chaplain and Chairman of our Spiritual Oversight Committee, thank you for undergirding me in prayer during this process and for the weekly prayer conference call. You are such a blessing to me!

To Dr. Glenda Glover, International President of our great sisterhood, thank you for the opportunity to serve as a member of the International Day of Prayer Committee under your administration. Thank you for exemplifying excellence in all that you do.

To Soror Sophia Nelson, my fellow Jersey Girl, thank you for always encouraging me to be my best version of me! You are the real deal, and I am grateful for your friendship.

To Soror Tonda Morgan, my childhood friend from elementary school, thank you for your constant optimism, words of encouragement, and prayers. You are indeed a great source of support, and I appreciate how God reconnected us.

To all the women praying for me and supporting me from the very start of this project – Dr. Nikki Westmoreland, Cecelia Toulson, a.k.a. "Rock Star", Elizabeth Carter, Rev. Denise Parker Lawrence, and Servant Tina Long; THANK YOU for being you!

To Coach Fard Bell, thank you for the extra push! I met you on the campus of Howard University over sixteen years ago as a college student, when I served

as the Baptist Chaplain. You were energetic, outgoing, and full of dreams and aspirations. Nothing has changed! I appreciate the man you have become and I am grateful to God for allowing our paths to cross again.

To Servant Tina Long, my friend, my sister/girlfriend, my sister in Christ, and my prayer partner. Your presence in my life has been simply remarkable! I treasure you for believing in me and for walking with me through this entire experience. Thank you for designing my cover and for serving as a part of my editorial team.

To my late father, Mr. Joseph M. Blair, Sr., I am grateful for his legacy and the love he showered me with while here on this earth. He always assured me that I could do anything I put my mind to do. I will forever be grateful to God for my daddy.

To my mother, Mrs. Gladys A. Blair, I am forever grateful that you allowed God to use you as a vessel to birth me into the world. You were also the first person to teach me how to pray. So many of the rich experiences afforded me in this life have been

because of the sacrifices you have made for me. We talk just about every day; and since I started this process of writing a book, every day you have asked me the same question, "Is the book finished yet?" I know it's your way of letting me know how proud you are of me. Thank you Mama, for being such a wonderful, beautiful, loving, and caring mother. I appreciate everything you have sacrificed for me and our entire family. I love you and thank God for allowing me to be your daughter.

To my brother, Joseph M. Blair, Jr. and his wife, Nina; my nieces, Jocelyn (Chris) Liggins, Tamara Edwards, and Mariaya Smith, my nephew, Evin Wallace, and my entire family, I love you so much for being my family. Thank you for your love and support.

I thank God daily for my husband, Reverend Ryan A. Wise. You have in your own creative way, inspired and nudged me to go on this journey. Your sacrifice, support, prayers, and love far exceed any words that I could possibly use to say thank you. I appreciate you for your dedication to our family and your work ethic; your encouragement has made this

day possible. I am forever grateful to God for our union, and I love you with all of my heart.

Finally, if I have overlooked saying thank you to anyone who has helped me in any way along this journey of writing this book, please charge it to my head and not my heart. I sincerely thank God for each and every one of you.

I love this quote,

> "I am not an expert on prayer.
> I am just a woman who prays."
> – Wendy Pope

FOREWORD

If the scriptures are correct, and I am sure that they are, the soul of man remains in a constant search for God. As the Creator searches for the creation, in a similar manner, we who are made by His hand can never be content until our hearts and our minds are at rest in Him.

Unfortunately, the lives we live are marked by distractions and disturbances that prevent us from the godly relationship we need. Moreover, the church is challenged to declare a word that is meaningful and relevant in a world of perverted politics and apostasy.

That is why the hymnologist was correct in asserting that this vile world will never lead us to God. That is what makes this prayerful and powerful offering by Reverend Adriane Blair Wise so important and necessary. It is important to know that this volume will not teach you to pray but it will bring you to your knees in a life of deeper devotion and consecration. **Teach Me, Lord**, **The Courage to Say No**, **Pregnant with Possibility**, and **Push Pause** are just a few of the prayer themes that will enrich your life.

I encourage you to read these words and to find yourself and your situation within them. You will find here more than a collection of words and miscellaneous thoughts. Instead, you will find a path to God and a sure touch of the Eternal. Read and pray with her and you will be blessed.

Dr. H. Beecher Hicks, Jr.
Senior Servant Emeritus
Metropolitan Baptist Church

PROLOGUE

Wise Women Pray is more than a book of prayers written by a woman who craves times in the presence of God. The purpose of my writing is simple; I desire to encourage someone to be all they were created to be. God has uniquely gifted each of us with an assignment to fulfill; to be of service in this world. However, too often we talk ourselves out of doing the very thing we were created to do. Perhaps doubt has gripped your heart, the fear of the unknown, or lack of self-confidence. Maybe procrastination has stifled your progress. Anyone of these can serve as the culprit that prevents you from taking the first step forward. But I challenge you, no I plead with you, do not delay any longer. As I write these words, I am also encouraging myself.

To the person reading this book, *Wise Women Pray* was written to remind you, you have something that someone else needs. You have a contribution, a gift, a talent, a skill, a story, a testimony, a solution, a remedy, a message, a poem, a song, a play, a blog, or even a prayer to offer. There is someone who is struggling with an issue, uncertain about a decision, standing at a crossroad, battling a disease, wrestling with a dilemma, fighting an addiction, or faced with a problem and you can help them. Whatever your contribution, don't put it off any longer. Go and do what only you can do. Someone is waiting to receive what you have to offer.

I have prayed about writing a book for a very long time. I have many interests, but prayer seems to be the one constant in my life where there is no deviation. It is such an intimate part of my journey. Perhaps that has been what has held me back from

sharing with others the full spectrum of my quiet moments in *His* presence. My conversations with God are so personal, so transparent, and so life-changing. I have hundreds of prayers tucked away in journals, on my cell phone, on my laptop, and on my home computer. I have post-it notes, 3x5 cards, and pieces of paper with prayers scribbled on them. On occasion, even a napkin had to suffice to capture what was in my heart at that moment. Some prayers are short, sweet and to the point, while others are lengthy lamentations. And then I have journals that I keep just to record what I'm grateful for throughout each day. That's probably one of my favorite things to do; to count my blessings, name them one by one! There are times when I can't sleep. I literally must get up and write out a prayer. Only then is the burden lifted and I'm able to rest.

Every so often I'm asked to write a prayer for a special occasion like a wedding or a house blessing, a publication, a special worship service, a family prayer, or dedication ceremony. These are the rare times I share what comes out of time spent in the presence of God. Several years back, I was gifted a book by the president of our prayer ministry at church, *Draw The Circle* by Mark Batterson. That book not only inspired me, but it made me uncomfortable; I felt like the Lord was telling me to do what he did. Write a book.

Several months after reading his book, I met him at a book signing in Silver Spring, Maryland, only to have him encourage me to treat the nudging to write a book as *holy and a prayer within itself.* Not being the only one, I have had other "nudging's" from family, friends, sorority sisters, and colleagues to write the book; the difference between being encouraged by others and Mark Batterson is he understood the trepidation I felt. He too wrestled with feelings of inadequacy, and talking to him made

what felt impossible, possible. I thought, "Maybe I do have something to offer!"

Today, I'm learning to face fear and do it anyway. To do what is hard; to do what is uncomfortable. Do it in spite of the unknown; to be faithful to the assignment of writing the book because God put it in my heart to do so. That is reason enough to do it, or anything else for that matter; because it pleases God. If no one ever reads this book, it will be well with my soul because it is out of a place of obedience that I write.

Over fifteen years ago while serving as the Baptist Chaplain on the campus of Howard University, I had a similar conversation over lunch with one of my preaching professors, the late Dr. Evans E. Crawford, Jr., Dean Emeritus of the Andrew Rankin Memorial Chapel. He spoke with me about the power of my "extemporaneous" prayer during the worship

experience that day. It was unrehearsed, it was unpolished, it was raw, but it was also heartfelt. His personal observation of that moment when I went before the throne room of grace was described using adjectives such conviction, passionate, and bold.

But then he shifted the conversation and asked if I would take him up on a challenge. He wanted me to put into practice the discipline of writing out prayers, "One never knows what will come of it" he said with a sheepish grin on his face. Because he was always so encouraging and affirming of anything I did in ministry, I would at least consider his request. I hadn't given much thought to the idea of writing out prayers before in the way he was speaking. I had some journals full of laments, SOS prayers, and poems. I prayed all the time, but writing them down conjured up feelings of vulnerability, after all, prayer is intimate.

You see, earlier that day I was given the privilege to provide the Centering Prayer during the Worship Service, a duty usually entrusted to the Dean of the Chapel. But on this particular Sunday, Dr. Bernard Richardson relinquished his duty to me. I was both humbled and horrified all at the same time because of the heaviness associated with the assignment. Dean Richardson was so eloquent, so polished, so pastoral; his words thoughtful, compassionate, and tender. His prayer was also usually written out, previous consideration given to the task at hand. But I had no prior notice to jot a few thoughts down. It was one of the most intimidating moments in my life. What most people didn't know about that day, Dean Richardson had just shared with me prior to service starting, that he received information about the radio broadcast – it had the number one listening audience in the area – something like 80,000 people tuning in every Sunday morning! Not only would those in the congregation hear my prayer, so would the listening

audience that tuned in week after week on 96.3 WHUR-FM radio! The pressure was on.

As I approached the microphone, I did so physically trembling but with bold confidence that the Holy Spirit would speak through me when I opened my mouth to speak to God on behalf of the people. I prayed like my life was on the line. I wanted God to know that I was putting my complete trust in His ability to meet the needs of His people. I wanted to say something to give those praying with me a hope to hold on just a little while longer; to know that we were praying to a God who loved and wanted the very best for their lives. This assignment was different from reading scripture like I had done on occasion before. I was administering a priestly function, serving as an intercessor, and representing the Dean who was the pastor to those who weekly pressed their way to chapel service or tuned in each Sunday morning.

That one prayer experience spurred a conversation over a meal with a man who challenged me to leave my land of familiar and to step into territory unknown. I didn't take up the discipline of writing prayers right away, but gradually over time, his challenge kept gnawing at my heart. And then one day, I purchased a journal, and I began to write and the Spirit led. After a while, I started typing out my prayers (I am a much faster typist) and like breathing, it became a necessity for my survival. I must spend time in His presence. I must commune with God. I must look to Him for help. I must incline my ear to hear God speak to me. My life depends on it.

I have chosen a variety of prayers; they were free of titles until I committed to sharing them in this book. Prayers like "Push Pause" and "Manifest" read like poetry, while others, "Teach Me, Lord", "Jesus Can Handle It" and "Keep on Praying" are litanies of sorts. Then there are prayers like "Give Me the

Courage to Say 'No" and "Pregnant with Possibility" which serve as my rendition of a lament. Each prayer is an outpouring of my dependence and trust in God and an expression of my love for Him. I really do love the Lord.

Until now, they have been locked away in journals for my private perusal and consumption. I release to share with others what I have held so dear and close to my heart. May *Wise Women Pray* fuel your desire to be all God is calling you to be. Perhaps these prayers will touch you in such a way that you too will be inspired to pen your own love letter(s) to God.

"Lord, teach us to pray."
– Luke 11:1

DAY 1

TEACH ME, LORD

Now it came to pass, as He was praying in a certain place, when He ceased, that one of His disciples said to Him, "Lord, teach us to pray, as John also taught his disciples."
– Luke 11:1

Today my prayer is simple – teach me, Lord!

Teach me, Lord, how to delight in Your presence.

Teach me, Lord, how to skillfully use Your Word.

Teach me, Lord, how to be led by Your Holy Spirit.

Teach me, Lord, how to wisely make decisions.

Teach me, Lord, how to worship You in spirit and in truth.

Teach me, Lord, how to praise You through the pain.

Teach me, Lord, how to practice what I preach.

Teach me, Lord, how to pray without ceasing.

Teach me, Lord, how to walk in obedience.

Teach me, Lord, how to hunger after righteousness.

Teach me, Lord, how to exercise humility.

Teach me, Lord, how to love without conditions.

Teach me, Lord, how to extend grace.

Teach me, Lord, how to forgive the unforgivable.

Teach me, Lord, how to believe in the miraculous.

Teach me, Lord, how to follow like a trustworthy disciple.

Teach me, Lord, how to be a receiver of good things.

Teach me, Lord, how to be an extravagant giver.

Teach me, Lord, how to be superlative in my service.

Teach me, Lord, how to steward my resources well.

Teach me, Lord, how to live an abundant life.

Teach me, Lord, how to patiently wait on You.

Teach me, Lord, how to be kind and gentle-hearted.

Teach me, Lord, how to demonstrate childlike faith.

Teach me, Lord, how to maximize my gifts.

Teach me, Lord, how to seize territory for Your Kingdom.
Teach me, Lord, how to discern Your voice in the midst of the noise.
Teach me, Lord, how to be courageous in the face of fear.
Teach me, Lord, how to be strong no matter the adversity.
Teach me, Lord, how to conduct my business affairs.
Teach me, Lord, how to live from a place of victory.

Thank You, Lord, for hearing my prayer and for giving me the strength and courage to live my life on purpose, according to Your perfect will. My heart is receptive and pliable to Your instructions. Through the power of Your Holy Spirit, I believe I will be able to do all things well.

I ask it all in the name of the Master Teacher, Jesus Christ. Amen.

DECLARATION

I am teachable.

What areas of your life do you need help with? Ask the Lord to teach you.

Growing up I loved reading books; learning new things intrigued me. My mother would on occasion, jokingly say, "Adriane, you are going to be a career student!" All jokes aside, I still love reading books, but I also enjoy sharing with others what I have learned. Information is meant to be shared. To do anything else is a waste and dishonorable to God.

DAY 2

TIME IN THE PRESENCE OF GOD

You will show me the path of life; in Your presence is fullness of joy; at Your right hand there are pleasures forevermore.
– Psalm 16:11

Help me to tune into Your voice, O God;

Your voice above the noise of this world.

Time alone in Your presence is reminiscent of Jesus;

Stealing away to be alone with You.

To a place of seclusion, Jesus prayed.

In the wilderness, He prayed.

Up to the mountain, He prayed.

In the Garden of Gethsemane, He prayed.

In those quiet moments, You, spoke to Jesus;

Providing instructions for His next move.

Jesus sought after You, God.

In humility and adoration, Jesus listened.

He heard.

He obeyed.

Speak God.

Your daughter is listening.

I desire to hear Your still, small voice.

Sitting in my dining room, I sit and wait.

My eyes are drawn to the activities of the outdoors.

As I gaze out of the window, clouds conceal the sun.

The snow begins to fall; Your majesty is seen in every flake.

In the distance, I notice geese playfully gliding across the yard.

Birds perched on tree limbs sing praises for an audience of One.

I eavesdrop on their worship, encouraged to join them in song.

The beauty of Your creation leaves me in a state of awe!

All nature acknowledges Your majesty!

It brings joy to my soul!

A smile breaks forth!

Laughter overtakes me!

My spirit is lifted!

My heart overflows with love for You!

I am appreciative.

I am grateful.

I am humbled.

O God, You, deserve the praise, the glory, and the honor.

Thank You, God, for time spent in Your presence.

In the precious name of Jesus, I pray.

Amen.

DECLARATION

I will spend time with God in prayer.

In the space below, write a prayer to God expressing your appreciation and gratitude.

Never forsake getting in the presence of God. In His presence you will find the answers to your questions, the solutions to your problems, the remedy for what ails you, and the peace to get you through life's storms.

DAY 3

I CAN RELY ON THE LORD

Praise the LORD, all you Gentiles! Laud Him, all you peoples! For His merciful kindness is great toward us, and the truth of the LORD endures forever. Praise the LORD!
– Psalm 117:1-2

Grateful for the morning nudge, I rejoice with the angels in singing Your praises, O Lord, for You, are worthy! You have been so merciful and kind to me. Your goodness surpasses my expectations. My portion of health, peace of mind, strength to endure, and the ability to navigate the trials that come with this life are made possible on account of You.

Lord, thank You, for the many ways in which You demonstrate Your reliability in my life:

When I fall on my knees before Your throne of grace, I can rely on You, to hear my prayers.

When I feel forsaken, I can rely on Your loving-kindness to reassure me, I am never alone.

When I need advice for my journey, I can rely on Your trustworthiness to guide me.

When I feel tired and weak, I can rely on Your supernatural power to reinvigorate my soul.

When I fall short of Your glory, I can rely on Your impartial correction and forgiveness.

When I am tempted to do things my way, I can rely on You, to show me the better portion.

When I stand in need of help, I can rely on You, to come see about me.

When I use my gifts and talents for Your glory, I can rely on You, for "good" success.

When I cry in the midnight hour, I can rely on You, to wipe my tears away.

When my resources are limited, I can rely on You, to exceed all that I could ask for or imagine.

When my body aches with pain, I can rely on You, to restore my health.
When the noise of this world is deafening, I can rely on Your still small voice to lead me.
When the evil one tries to derail my plans, I can rely on You, to order my steps.
When the burdens of this life are too great, I can rely on You, to do the heavy lifting.
When the enemy comes to eat up my flesh, I can rely on You, to protect me from the devour.
When the storm is raging in my life, I can rely on You, to see me through it, or calm me in it.
When the warfare is intense, I can rely on You, to fight my battles as I rest in You.
When fear and doubt try to overtake me, I can rely on You, to renew my strength and courage.
When life feels desolate and dry, I can rely on You, to cause living waters to flow in my direction.

Once again, from the bottom of my heart thank You, Lord, for being so reliable. I truly appreciate all that You do. I love You, Lord, and I ask it all in the name of Jesus. Amen.

DECLARATION

I can rely on the Lord.

What area(s) in your life, do you need to rely on the Lord? Write it in the space below; then submit it to God in prayer.

As you go about your day,
remember God is gracious, loving,
and kind.

DAY 4

TURN EVERY CARE INTO A PRAYER

Be anxious for nothing, but in everything by prayer and supplication, with thanksgiving, let your requests be made known to God; and the peace of God, which surpasses all understanding, will guard your hearts and minds through Christ Jesus.
– Philippians 4:6-7

Hezekiah received the letter from the messengers and read it. Then he went up to the temple of the LORD and spread it out before the LORD. And Hezekiah prayed to the LORD: "LORD Almighty, the God of Israel, enthroned between the cherubim, you alone are God over all the kingdoms of the earth. You have made heaven and earth. Give ear, LORD, and hear; open your eyes, LORD, and see; listen to all the words Sennacherib has sent to ridicule the living God."
– Isaiah 37:14-17 (NIV)

Almighty God, I am so thankful for Your Word, and the nuggets You drop into my lap each day. I appreciate how You orchestrate the meeting of my problems with Your solutions. I am grateful for the richness of Your Word. As I meditate on the Scriptures, I take to heart the words of the Apostle Paul who admonishes us, "Be anxious for nothing, but in everything by prayer and supplication, with thanksgiving, let your requests be made known to God; and the peace of God, which surpasses all understanding, will guard your hearts and minds through Christ Jesus" (Philippians 4:6-7).

The Prophet Isaiah also tells the story of King Hezekiah; when he was threatened by his enemies, Hezekiah brought his cares before You God, "… he went up to the temple of the LORD and spread it out before the LORD" (Isaiah 37:15). Even though he was the king, he humbled himself before the King of Kings, and he drew closer to You to receive instructions. He prayed, and You listened. He asked You for help, and the very night he asked, You, answered. You responded, **because Hezekiah prayed**! You rescued and delivered both Hezekiah and his people from the hands of their enemies. I praise You, for the testimony of Hezekiah! It serves as good news for me today as I lay before You all of my cares, troubles, concerns, and issues.

I submit to You, Lord, the enemy of debt and lack that attempts to stifle our ability to care for our family and the work of ministry. Your Word reminds me You are the God, "Who is able to do exceedingly abundantly above all that we can ask or think" (Ephesians 3:20). It also says, "And my God shall supply all your needs according to His riches in glory by Christ Jesus" (Philippians 4:19). According to Deuteronomy 15:6, "For the LORD God will bless you just as He promised you; you shall lend to many nations, but you shall not borrow . . ." As we take heed to Your instructions, "Bring all the tithe into the storehouse . . ." we wait for You to ". . . open the windows of heaven and pour out for *us* such blessing that there will not be room enough to receive it" (Malachi 3:10). Please, help us Lord, to steward well everything You have given to us.

I submit to You, Lord, the enemy of discord that would keep us at odds with one another. The Bible says, "Can two walk together, unless they are agreed?" (Amos 3:3); please help us to walk together in agreement. As we strive to "Abide in Christ, so Christ can abide in us" (John 15:4), help us to be ". . . quick to hear, slow to speak, and slow to anger" (James 1:19). Give us an ear to hear wise counsel; surround us with godly friends and associates as we strive to make life-affirming choices. Provide us with wholesome and edifying experiences that speak of Your goodness in our lives. Impart to us the necessary wisdom, knowledge, and understanding to discern the shifts in seasons in our lives.

I submit to You, Lord, the enemy of sickness and disease that has come against many members of our family. As I trust You to be our Great Physician, I do so believing, "The wounds of Christ have healed us; Jesus also bore our sins that we would die to sin and live for righteousness" (1 Peter 2:24).

Regardless of the doctor's report, I choose to agree with Your Word, as I stand on it as my profession of faith. You have designed our bodies as temples to house Your Holy Spirit; through His power, we need assistance in caring for them. Help us to eat foods that only add nutritional value to our bodies. Equip us with the appropriate information to practice preventive care before sickness ever appears. Raise our awareness to behaviors and habits we may be doing unintentionally, that would sabotage our efforts to be healthy and whole. Break the appeal of unhealthy living practices that would keep us enslaved and dependent on anything other than You.

Thank You, Lord, for hearing my plea for help.

Thank You, for intervening and for dealing with all of my enemies. Just like You rescued Hezekiah and his people, I trust You will do the same for us. May someone else be encouraged as I bear witness to what You have done for me, You, are also able to do for them; if they would but pray, as we have been instructed to do in Your Word.

I ask it all in the name of Jesus, the One who makes all of my enemies, tremble and flee. Amen.

DECLARATION

I will turn every care into a prayer.

What "enemies" are you facing in your life today? Write them down and entrust that God will deal with them as you follow the example of Hezekiah.

Remember, Jesus said, "Come to Me, all who are weary and heavy-laden, and I will give you rest" (Matthew 11:28).

Rest in His promise, knowing you can tell your mountain about the bigness of your God.

DAY 5

NEW BEGINNINGS

Behold, I will do a new thing, now it shall spring forth; shall you not know it? I will even make a road in the wilderness and rivers in the desert.
– Isaiah 43:19

Gracious and Eternal God, with adoration in our hearts and praise on our lips, we thank You for seeing us through another year. As we transition into the New Year, we are reminded that You are "the same yesterday, today, and forevermore" (Hebrews 13:8), "You are unchanging" (Malachi 3:6), and that "You make all things new" (Revelation 21:5).

Lord, we confess we have "fallen short of Your glory" (Romans 3:23) and need Your grace and

mercy as we enter into this New Year. We also confess our need for more of You:

More of Your unconditional love;
More of Your patience;
More of Your mercy;
More of Your grace;
More of Your kindness;
More of Your humility;
More of Your meekness;
More of Your joy;
More of Your forgiveness;
and more of Your peace.

Lord, we need the power of Your Holy Spirit to direct our steps for this new season. Please help us to put our entire trust in You, "Leaning not on our own understanding, but in all our ways acknowledging You in all that we say and do" (Proverbs 3:5-6). According to Proverbs 3:9-10, help us, "To honor You with our possessions, and with the first-fruits of

all our increase; so that our barns will be filled with plenty, and our vats will overflow with new wine." Lord, anoint us afresh; give us supernatural power to live in such a way that we bring glory and honor to Your Holy name. Help us to daily crucify our flesh, to die to self so that we may fully live for You. Give us the ability to exemplify the teachings of our Lord and Savior Jesus Christ, as we declare, "Not our will but Your will be done" (Luke 22:42).

Lord, we ask for You to "encamp Your angels" (Psalm 34:7) around us, protecting us from all forms of hurt, harm, and danger. Give us wisdom and discernment to quickly recognize the attempts of the evil one to lead us into temptation; "deliver us from the snares" devised for our destruction (Psalm 91:3). We are grateful for the "sufficiency of Your grace" (2 Corinthians 12:9), for "not putting more on us than we can handle" (1 Corinthians 10:13), and for being our "burden bearer" (Psalm 68:19).

Lord, we also ask for the grace to be the type of people who "care about the needs of others" (Philippians 2:4). Help us to have a reputation as generous givers, as we follow the instructions of Luke 6:37-38, "To give, and it will be given to us; good measure, pressed down, shaken together, running over, will be put into our laps. For with the measure we use it will be measured back to us."

Help us to be exceptional servant leaders and lovers of Your people. As we submit our hopes and dreams into Your capable hands, we trust You to "prosper the plans" You have designed specifically for us to achieve (Jeremiah 29:11). Sanctify our souls and set a standard of excellence in us that brings honor to Your name. Shine Your light bright in our lives, as we work to make a difference in our world.

Lord, thank You, for giving us the "desires of our hearts and for making all our plans succeed" (Psalm 20:4).

Thank You, for the "new thing You are doing in our lives" (Isaiah 43:18).

Thank You, for giving us the courage to obey Your instructions and for the benefits that follow.

Thank You, for Holy Ghost revelation, insight, and understanding as we move forward into unknown territory.

We love You, God, we praise Your Holy name, and we ask it all in the name of Your Son, Jesus Christ. Amen.

DECLARATION

I embrace new beginnings.

As you embrace the new, what old things do you need to release? Perhaps, you have habits that no longer serve you well or thought patterns that have kept you stuck in the past; whatever it is, surrender it to God.

"If you want to improve your life immediately, clean out a closet. Often it's what we hold onto that holds us back."
– Cheryl Richardson

DAY 6

MANIFEST

You will also declare a thing, and it will be established for you; so light will shine on your ways.
– Job 22:28

Gracious and Eternal God, as I worship You this morning, in spirit and in truth, I am so grateful for the possibilities that await me.

Grateful for birthing rights.
Grateful that I am a work in progress.
Grateful that I am becoming who You designed me to be.

I declare Your promises to me shall be fulfilled.

Oh, Lord, I desire for You to manifest wonderful things in my life!

Manifest, Your love.
Manifest, Your peace.
Manifest, Your joy.
Manifest, Your wisdom.
Manifest, Your kindness.
Manifest, Your meekness.
Manifest, Your strength.
Manifest, Your creativity.
Manifest, Your ideas.
Manifest, Your favor.
Manifest, Your mercy.
Manifest, Your grace.
Manifest, Your healing.
Manifest, Your courage.
Manifest, Your power.
Manifest, Your abundant blessings.

Manifest!

Manifest!

Manifest!

Manifest, all for the sake of Your glory in my life! Manifest more of You in my life so others may see less of me!

I decree it and declare it, in the marvelous name of Jesus. Amen.

DECLARATION

I trust God to manifest good things in my life.

What are you praying for God to manifest in your life today?

Your eyes are being opened to all the wonderful possibilities around you. What a privilege to be entrusted to birth something for God!

DAY 7

WHEN LOVE IS THE NECESSARY ANTIDOTE

And above all things have fervent love for one another, for "love will cover a multitude of sins."
– 1 Peter 4:8

Good Morning, Lord! I'm grateful for another day of new mercies. Thank You, for the privilege of talking directly with You, about my desires, my aspirations, my joys, my heartaches, and my sorrows.

Lord, in recent days I've experienced disappointment, betrayal, and even the sting of hurtful words from unexpected people; people whom I regarded as safe, secure, and friendly. But I was blindsided by their behavior, rendered speechless. I know it's been said, "hurt people, hurt people" and

You can attest to the validity of this statement so much better than me. You are familiar with the hurtful words of so-called friends and bona fide foes. You have tasted the bitter cup of betrayal from within Your inner circle. You, understand all too well how serving people can sometimes cause disappointment – so I run to You, for refuge.

Lord, I ask You to deal with those who have been unkind to me, who have spoken harshly to me, and who have regarded my kindness as weakness. Protect my heart from re-injury, and from the infectious spread of things like contention, resentment, contempt, and discord. As I submit to Your Lordship, I need the power of the Holy Spirit, to bridle my tongue. Please give me the necessary grace to endure and not retaliate; to use words of wisdom when communicating, harboring no ill will or bitterness in my heart.

Your instructions are clear, "Love your enemies, bless those who curse you, do good to those who hate you, and pray for those who spitefully use you and persecute you" (Matthew 5:44). So in obedience to Your Word, I forgive those who have hurt me, just as I trust You, to forgive me when I fall short of Your glory; when I have sinned against You. Please be merciful in Your chastisement; repair the breach in our relationships, and give me beauty for my ashes. With a humble heart, I open myself to the overflow of Your unconditional love, that love that covers a multitude of sins.

Thank You, Lord, for exposing the works of the devil, the accuser, for "The thief does not come except to steal, and to kill, and to destroy" (John 10:10a). Thank You, for the reminder that my fight is not with my brother or my sister, that this warfare is spiritual, "For we do not wrestle against flesh and blood, but against principalities, against powers, against the rulers of the darkness of this age, against spiritual hosts of wickedness in the heavenly places" (Ephesians 6:12).

So, I stand, having my armor on, trusting that You, are fighting my battles as I submit everything to You, in prayer. I believe, what the enemy meant for evil, You, will use it for my good, and for Your glory. I ask it all in the name of the One, who secured my salvation and victory by defeating Satan, death, and the grave, with His resurrection power, Jesus the Christ. Amen.

DECLARATION

I choose to walk in love and forgiveness.

So, whom might you need to forgive or demonstrate unconditional love toward?

Forgiveness frees you of the burden of harboring feelings you weren't designed to carry. Free your heart of any bitterness, anger, and resentment; do it as an act of obedience to God, do it to secure your peace of mind, and do it for your own happiness and contentment. Remember, those who are least deserving of your love and forgiveness usually need it the most.

"It's not your heart that hurts, but love. And it is love itself that contains the most powerful medicine."
– Author Unknown

DAY 8

THE FAST THAT GOD CHOOSES

Is this not the fast that I have chosen: to loose the bonds of wickedness, to undo the heavy burdens, to let the oppressed go free, and that you break every yoke?
– Isaiah 58:6

Gracious and Eternal God, orchestrator of all things good in my life, I humbly come before Your throne of grace once again with a spirit of gratitude for how You care for me and my entire family. I am grateful for this season of fasting for a breakthrough and for the truth of Your Word. As You, teach me about the power of fasting and prayer, I desire to participate in a fast that You choose.

Father, God, in accordance with Isaiah 58:8-14, I agree with Your Word, and receive the glorious

promises on behalf of myself and my family, as I apply the disciplines of fasting and prayer.

Thank You, Lord, for the ability to see clearly as You bring us into the marvelous light.

Thank You, for our health which springs forth speedily – physically, spiritually, emotionally, and mentally.

Thank You, for the confidence and assurance of knowing that You will always guide us along the path You have chosen.

Thank You, for satisfying our every need regardless of the issues of this world.

Thank You, for giving us life that is abundantly blessed.

Thank You, for being a never ending source of inspiration and blessings in our lives.

Thank You, for allowing us to be builders of that which appears to be ruins and desolation.

Thank You, for affording us the opportunity to discover pillars to build our lives and the community in which we serve.
Thank You, for calling us repairers of broken walls, streets, and houses.
Thank You, for equipping and empowering us to create and provide a place of protection and safety for those within our sphere of influence.
Thank You, for answering our prayers when we call on You for help in our time of need.

Father, God, please strengthen us during this season to stay true to our commitment to fast, to pray, and to do good to people that are unable to repay us. Asking it all in the name of Your Son, our Savior and Lord, Jesus Christ. Amen.

DECLARATION

I am dedicated to the fast that God chooses.

Read Isaiah 58, allowing the Holy Spirit to minister to you about the text. Now read it a second time and underline the benefits offered to you when you adhere to the fast that God chooses. What area of your life do you need a breakthrough?

"Ask for what you want and be prepared to get it!"
– Dr. Maya Angelou

DAY 9

THE COURAGE TO SAY "NO"

I have come that they may have life, and that they may have it more abundantly.
– John 10:10b

Almighty God, I approach Your throne of grace, with a humble heart. Grateful for this day, I confess my dependency on You. This season of spiritual growth has taught me some valuable lessons, especially as it pertains to the use of the word "no." Lord, sometimes saying "no" really does take more courage than saying "yes."

At times, my desire to please people or to not disappoint them has gotten in the way of me pleasing You. Sometimes, it has even made it difficult to remain true to me.

So, as I desire to live an authentic life, please give me the courage to say “no.”

“No” to contentious conversations.

“No” to discriminatory practices.

“No” to dream-killers.

“No” to energy-zappers.

“No” to fruitless activities.

“No” to growth obstructers.

“No” to irrelevant undertakings.

“No” to needless nonsense.

“No” to purposeless ponderings.

“No” to chaos and confusion.

“No” to trivial pursuits.

“No” to unproductive behavior.

“No” to phony people.

“No” to unhealthy associations.

“No” to disorganization.

“No” to entanglements.

“No” to idleness.

“No” to intimidation.

“No” to oppression.

“No” to procrastination.

“No” to self-doubt.

“No” to fear.

I say “no” to anything or anyone devised to disrupt, derail, or destroy my destiny.

Courageously, I ask it all in the name of the One that came that I may have life and that I may have it more abundantly, Jesus the Christ. Amen.

DECLARATION

To the things that no longer serve me well,
I have the courage to say “no.”

Take some time to write down every area in your life that you need courage to say "no."

Saying "no" really is an option, in response to a request made of you. We have a Helper in the form of the Holy Spirit to guide us through the difficult terrain of life. Ask for wisdom and discernment and then trust the Holy Spirit to guide you in your decision-making.

DAY 10

TRUSTING GOD WITH MY DAY

The LORD is my strength and my shield; my heart trusted in Him, and I am helped; therefore my heart greatly rejoices, and with my song I will praise Him.
– Psalm 28:7

Father, God, thank You, for the gift of another day of life. I glorify Your Holy name, for You, are so worthy to be praised. This morning, I did not jump up out of the bed as usual. Instead, I laid in the bed with my eyes wide open, taking in my surroundings. As the familiar came into focus, my attention was drawn to my breathing; I am alive another day! Hallelujah!

Thanks to You, I can hear the pounding of my heart. Everything is so still and quiet; the silence is almost

deafening. Then the sound of running water alerts me that someone else is up too. A car can be heard passing by in the distance, and then another one; my neighbors are heading out early in spite of the bitter cold temperatures. The calm I experienced when I first awoke is quickly dissipating into a memory, as thoughts begin to flood my mind of the unfolding of my day.

Lord, I am not sure what this day will bring. What I am confident of is I must trust You, to be with me as I go about doing what has been entrusted to me: a family to care for, a mother to call, a friend to check on, a bed to be made, meals to fix, dishes to clean, floors to sweep, carpets to vacuum, and clothes to be washed. I have meetings to attend, assignments to complete, phone calls to return, people to encourage, prayers to be lifted, and lessons to be prepared. These are the things that I know about.

But for the unknowns of this day – the interruptions, the unexpected phone call, the possible delay, or the unmet need to be filled. Please give me the grace to deal with anything that comes my way. I am depending on the intercession of Jesus. I am yielding to the guidance of Your Holy Spirit; and I am leaning on Your understanding to see me through it all, Lord.

Thank You, God, for listening to my musings this morning. As I sit and wait for You to speak, my ear is bent toward heaven, my heart is receptive to instruction, and my eyes are focused on You. I rejoice in knowing that You are with me, and I will praise You, throughout this day for Your goodness towards me. I love You, God, and I thank You, for being so good to me. It is in the matchless name of Jesus Christ, I pray. Amen.

Addendum: As I finished typing this prayer, I received a text message from a member of the church. She asked for prayer for an upcoming surgery.

Lord, I petition You on behalf of my sister in Christ, calling on You as the Great Physician. Please give her Your perfect peace as she prepares to undergo this surgical procedure. Bless the medical team who will perform the surgery; please use them as instruments of healing and restoration. Give the surgeon precision of hand, knowledge, and discernment to successfully accomplish the assignment. Thank You for protecting her from any complications, clotting, or infections during this operation. In the name of Jesus, who is her Strength, Redeemer, and Healer, I pray. Amen.

DECLARATION

I will trust God with my day.

Make a list of every assignment, appointments, meetings, etc., you have scheduled for this day. Once you have made your list, submit it to God, in prayer, trusting that He will guide and direct you throughout the day.

Make it a daily practice to submit
Your day to the Lord.

DAY 11

I WANT TO BE A GIVER

But this I say: He who sows sparingly will also reap sparingly, and he who sows bountifully will also reap bountifully. So let each one give as he purposes in his heart, not grudgingly or of necessity; for God loves a cheerful giver.
– 2 Corinthians 9:6-7

Heavenly Father, thank You for giving me the greatest Gift of all, Your Only Begotten Son, the One who secured my salvation. As I die to self and live for You, Lord, please help me to be a giver:

A giver of worship, that brings glory and honor to Your name.
A giver of praise and adoration, that exemplifies Your greatness.
A giver of gratitude, for the many ways You have blessed my life.

A giver of hope, to those who have lost their way.
A giver of words, that are positive, life-affirming, and build up the cause of Christ.
A giver of wise counsel, for someone who is done with foolish pursuits.
A giver of love, that conceals the sins of my brothers and sisters.
A giver of kindness, that considers the needs of others.
A giver of compassion, for the marginalized and forgotten.
A giver of comfort, to someone experiencing loss.
A giver of patience, to the person least deserving of it.
A giver of fidelity, to my partner in marriage.
A giver of loyalty, to the call on my life.
A giver of compliments, to the person who rarely receives recognition.
A giver of encouragement, to the kid struggling with low self-confidence.

A giver of information, to the student eager to expand the borders of their mind.

A giver of friendship, to the one desirous of a friend.

A giver of hugs, to someone desperately yearning physical tough.

A giver of empathy, to the person who feels insignificant and invisible.

A giver of strength, to those who feel like giving up.

A giver of laughter, to brighten someone's day.

A giver of generosity, to a mother who can never repay me.

A giver of time, to the friend who needs a listening ear.

I ask it all in the name of the greatest Giver of all, Jesus the Christ. Amen.

DECLARATION

I am a giver of good things.

As you meditate on the goodness of God in your own life, what do you have that you could give to someone today?

"We are at our best when we are giving. In fact, we are most like God when we are giving."
– Max Lucado

DAY 12

RESTORATION OF OUR MARRIAGES

And now abide faith, hope, love, these three; but the greatest of these is love.
– 1 Corinthians 13:13

Gracious and Eternal God, we need our Heavenly Father today to step into our marriages; we need the tender, loving care of a sovereign God. Lord, we are forever grateful to You, for the strategy to fight for what rightfully belongs to us. There are things that have been devised to undermine our marriages, so we cry out to You. We take a knee, believing by faith, that the victory is already ours.

Father, we know Your Word says in Amos 3:3, "Can two walk together, unless they are agreed?" We also

know in marriage it actually takes 'three' to agree, for us to be successful; we need You, and each other. Lord, we are imperfect, therefore making our marriages imperfect. But we know when we add a perfect God to the equation, all things are possible for those who believe; please help our unbelief. God, we believe that You can breathe on our imperfect unions, and bring resurrection power to them in such a way that they can live again. Father, we believe You can perfect us. According to Psalm 51:10, "Create in ***us*** a clean heart, O God; and renew a right spirit within ***us***." We intentionally use the words of agreement when speaking to each other, like *we*, *us*, *our* and *together*, as we desire to partner with each other in this mystery called marriage.

We need You, Father, to touch our hearts to be receptive to Your Word, to open our ears to hear Your voice, and to open our eyes to see Your spiritual truths. Help us to also obey Your

instructions accordingly, as we demonstrate our desire to please You. Help us to put away childish behavior, to walk upright in integrity and good character. Let our words be true and exemplify the teachings of our Lord and Savior.

We need You, Father, to show us how to communicate openly and honestly with one another, even when it's difficult and uncomfortable to do so. Give us the articulation of our lips and clarity of thought, when talking to each other. May we be respectful in our conversations, always giving consideration to the other person, not only in what we say, but also in how we say it.

We need You, Father, to help us to put away worldly ways of handling conflict – things like withholding love, walking around in anger, being easily offended, not giving each other the benefit of the doubt, being unforgiving, and living selfishly. Instead, show us

how to walk in love, to be slow to anger, not be so easily offended, and always open for reconciliation; to quickly forgive each other, and to put the others needs above our own.

We need You, Father, to soften hardened hearts and transform thoughts of negativity; help us to meditate on these things, "Whatever things are true, whatever things are noble, whatever things are just, whatever things are pure, whatever things are lovely, whatever things are of good report, if there is any virtue and if there is anything praiseworthy. . ." (Philippians 4:8). Make our hearts pliable and receptive to be doers of Your Word.

We need You, Father, to help us to make You, our first priority and then to be each other's top priority, putting no other person (children, parents, siblings, relatives, or friends) above each other or anything or any activity (jobs, businesses, church, ministry,

military, sorority, fraternity, community service, school, sports, or hobbies).

We need You, Father, to teach us how to build a home together; a place where Your Spirit abides. To share in caring for the needs of our home – maintenance and upkeep, purchasing furniture, decorating, and creating an environment that makes everyone at peace and welcome in the space.

We need You, Father, to help us to use wisdom and not foolishness as pertains to our finances; to be good stewards of all of our resources – to pay our bills on time, to use credit cards wisely, to pay off all debt in a timely manner, to save, and to invest in kingdom initiatives. As we submit our tithes and offerings to You, thank You, for allowing us to put You to the test; for throwing open your windows of heaven, and for pouring out a blessing that there shall not be room enough to receive it. (Malachi 3:10). All we need is

one blessing to turn our situations around! Thank You, for abundant overflow in our lives and for the manifold blessings that allow us to be blessings to others.

We need You, Father, to help us as we humble ourselves to do self-evaluation concerning things that we may do that have become habits that are annoying and chipping away at our marriages. Destroy every work of the devil that would keep us focused on our shortcomings; help us to look past one another's faults and to see one another's need for patience, kindness, compassion, support, and unconditional love. Help us not to be chief critic of our spouses or of ourselves. Help us to use our words only to build up, to affirm, and to encourage our spouses. When the urge to tear down, speak harshly, or discourage in anyway rises up in us, we give you permission to put a bridle on our mouths and to arrest our thoughts!

We need You, Father, to help us to be more caring about one another as pertains to our sexual needs and desires; step into our intimate places and bring us to a place of *agape* and *eros* love – to be more compassionate, affectionate, tender-hearted, and loving. Bring romance back into our relationships; stir up our passion for one another, show us how to court each other, to shower one another with words of affirmation, with gifts, and deeds that solidify our love for one another.

We need You, Father, to help us to be mindful of what we feed our spirit, the things that we deem as entertainment; the things we read, watch, listen to, and look at – books, magazines, movies, music, even conversations – anything that would cause division within our relationship, lead us astray, or cause a breach within our marriages. Sanctify our souls and give us an appetite for wholesome, edifying and

godly things that build us up as couples and bring us into a closer relationship with You.

We need You, Father, to touch our hearts to be open to correction, to be quick to forgive, to admit when we are wrong, and to be okay with saying "I'm sorry," "please forgive me," or "I forgive you." Bind every spirit of stubbornness, defiance, rebellion, and refusal to submit to Your will and purpose for our marriages. Loose us to walk in humility, submission, surrender, and obedience to Your will and way.

We need You, Father, to teach us how to fight fair, to handle conflict and disagreement with godly precepts and teachings in mind; to work through our problems and not use the threat of separation and/or divorce as a means of resolving conflict. To be open to receive godly counsel when necessary; and to partner with other couples who will serve to keep us accountable to each other and to You. Raise up

mighty men of valor and mighty women of virtue, men and women who can speak a word of correction into our lives. Break every yoke that would keep us bound to old ways of thinking, and reacting to problems or challenges; show us how to respond, tempered by Your Spirit in a more loving and considerate way.

We need You, Father, to teach us how to reconcile our differences, instead of recoiling and shutting down, or retreating to other parts of the house or sleeping in separate bedrooms; mature us, perfect us, and make us fully grown in You, Lord. Heal any brokenness in us. Remove any residual hurt and pain from past relationships, or even childhood trauma that we experienced that keeps us stuck in the past. Loose the chains of torment and give us Your perfect peace.

We need You, Father, to destroy any obsession of the heart over someone other than our spouses; sever any relationships that would compromise the health and wellness of our marriages. Break every soul-tie, and destroy every wicked scheme devised for the destruction of our marriages. Reposition us to go into the enemy's territory and take back everything he has stolen from us. Take us to another level in You, so that we can bear witness to others that You are no respecter of persons, that our relationships can be healed and restored too; what You have done for one, You, can also do it for others.

We need You, Father, to help us to hold onto Your unchanging hand; to believe that You are the God of miracles who can restore, revive, reconcile, reignite, resurrect, and make brand new our love for one another. Help us to put our hope in You, for "You are well able to do exceedingly abundantly above all that we ask or think, according to the power that

works in us" (Ephesians 3:20). Remind us daily that we are "More than conquerors through Christ who loved us" (Romans 8:37), and to speak over our marriage the words of the Prophet, Isaiah, "No weapon that is formed against us shall prosper; and every tongue that rises against us in judgment shall be condemned" (54:17). We are "The redeemed of the Lord, and we say so, because You have redeemed us from the hand of the enemy" (Psalm 107:2).

Thank You, Father, for hearing this prayer!
Thank You, for the blood of Jesus that covers us!
Thank You, for the power of Your Holy Spirit dwelling within us!
Thank You, for correction, comfort, and guidance!
Thank You, for destroying the works of the enemy!
Thank You, for equipping us with the necessary tools!
Thank You, for healing and deliverance!
Thank You, for the spirit of agreement!

Thank You, for supernatural provision!

Thank You, for angelic reinforcement!

Thank You, for unconditional love!

Thank You, for ordering our steps!

Thank You, for unmerited favor!

Thank You, for understanding!

Thank You, for knowledge!

Thank You, for protection!

Thank You, for wisdom!

Thank You, for peace!

Thank you, for grace!

Thank You, for joy!

Father, we want our marriages to bring glory, honor, and praise to Your Holy name! We want our marriages to be fruitful for the sake of Your Kingdom! We ask it all in the wonderful, mighty name of our Lord and Savior, Jesus Christ. Amen.

[This prayer was written to edify and encourage the members of the Marriage Enrichment Ministry at Metropolitan Baptist Church in Largo, Maryland.]

Note: This prayer is inspired by a book I have had for some time now but never got past reading the first three pages. It's written by Stormie Omartian and it is entitled, *The Power of Prayer to Change Your Marriage.* As I reviewed the Table of Contents and read each chapter title (14 to be exact), I immediately became dismayed by the heaviness of each category. But then the Holy Spirit quickened in my spirit to be still, stay calm, and align my thoughts accordingly; to take the knowledge that I just obtained and use it to my advantage… remember "people perish for lack of knowledge." (Hosea 4:6).

It is our responsibility to use wisdom in order to counteract the devil's tactics designed for the destruction of our marriages. I do my best fighting in my prayer closet, submitting everything into the hands of God, who promises not only to fight my battles, but guarantees my victories! I know all too well from previous experiences, that operating in my flesh will only make matters worse. So I had to consciously decide to *get out of my own way*, surrender my desire to stay in a broken, hurt place, and allow the Holy Spirit to step in and guide me in praying this prayer for every marriage that stands in need of

enrichment. I am forever grateful to God for the strategy to fight for what rightfully belongs to me and I hope and pray some other couple will be strengthened in their marriage. I look forward to reading the other 250 pages of her book, but in the meantime, I'm going to be thankful for the Table of Contents!

DECLARATION

I declare our marriage is strong.

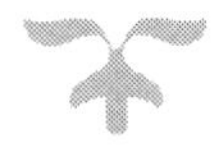

Regardless of your marital status, is there a relationship that you are engaged in (spouse, friend, family member, co-worker, etc.) that could benefit from God's guidance? Share the details below and submit the relationship to God in prayer.

Sometimes you may feel like the demands of marriage are too hard and you may want to throw in the towel. I admonish you, don't give up. Instead, secure your anchor to the covenant you made to your spouse and to God. Put your trust in the God of the covenant.

"Marriage is still a good idea because it is God's idea. He created it. He designed it. He established it and defined the parameters.... Marriage is of divine origin."
– Myles Munroe

DAY 13

GOD LISTENS TO ME

Depend on the LORD; trust Him, and He will take care of you.
– Psalm 37:5 (NCV)

Lord, I have need of You.
I have turned off everything.
The music is off.
The television is off.
The ringer on my phone is off.
Social media and email, both are shut down.
I need silence.
I need to speak to my Heavenly Father.
I need to talk to my, Abba.
When I speak, You, listen to me.
What I have to say matters to You.
My voice matters.
My words matter.
My feelings matter.
My tears matter.

My pain matters.
My disappointment matters.
My dreams matter.
My happiness matters.
My joy matters.
It all matters to You.
What does not matter is the size of my problem.
No care is insignificant.
No trouble too big.
You are so attentive.
So gracious and kind.
I feel heard.
I feel cared for.
I feel loved.
You hear my prayers.
My prayers even matter to You.
To think, my prayers activate movement in the heavenly realm.
My faith gets Your attention.
You even take notice of my mustard seed faith.
I am grateful.
I am humbled.
I am inspired.
I am in awe.
Lord, thank You, for listening.

I have an ear to hear.
I now wait patiently to hear from You.
What do You want to say to me, Lord?

> I can *depend on You.*
> I can *trust You.*
> *You will take care of me.*

Thank You, for answering me.
Thank You, for being so dependable.
Thank You, for being so trustworthy.
Thank You, for being so caring.
Lord, thank You, for the reassurance of Your love for me.
I rest in You.

Asking it all in Jesus' mighty name. Amen.

DECLARATION

God listens to me because I matter to Him.

Can you remember a time when you felt like you were talking but no one was listening? When you talk to God you never have to worry about feeling unheard. Shut off all the noise around you and spend some time in silence. Share your heart with God. Allow Him to speak to you through His Word. Write down what is revealed to you in the space below.

Allow yourself to be a good listener of God and of other people. Everyone desires to be heard.

DAY 14

PUSH PAUSE

For unto us a Child is born, unto us a Son is given: and the government shall be upon His shoulders. And His name shall be called, Wonderful, Counselor, Mighty God, Everlasting Father, Prince of Peace.
– Isaiah 9:6

My Lord, and my God,

I choose to push pause today.

To stop the hustle and bustle of doing,

And instead, focus on just being.

Rapt in Your presence.

Basking in Your glory.

Inclined to Your voice.

Enveloped by Your love.

Filled with Your peace.

Recipient of Your mercy.

Trusting in Your timing.

Grace abounding.

Refreshing.

Renewal.

Revival.

All mine for the asking.

My Lord, and my God,

I choose to push pause today.

No pondering about what's next.

Simply soaking up this moment.

Satisfied to spend it with You.

Your name shall be called,

Wonderful,

Counselor,

Mighty God,

Everlasting Father,

Prince of Peace.

Jesus.

My Lord.

My Savior.

I pray.

Amen.

DECLARATION

I choose to push pause today.

Take a moment to "Push Pause" in your own life. Find a quiet spot to read and meditate on one Bible verse. Write down what thoughts come to mind and then entrust it to God.

You will never regret the time you spend with God in prayer.

DAY 15

LORD, I NEED YOUR WISDOM

"Jesus increased in wisdom, stature and favor with man and with God."
– Luke 2:52

Gracious and Eternal God, my love for You is abounding as I meditate on Your unconditional love for me. The mercy and unmerited grace You extend to me daily keeps me in a posture of humility and gratitude. As I bask in Your splendor this morning, I yield to Your will and purpose for my life. Oh how I love You, and magnify Your Holy name.

I act on Your Word today and commit to agreeing with Luke 2:52, that like Jesus, "I increase in wisdom, and stature, and favor with man and with

God." I believe You will do it for me. Lord, You, owe me nothing, but you give me everything.

Lord, thank You, for increasing my wisdom; to know how to handle every situation that comes my way; I need Your wisdom to figure it all out! In my own strength I will fail, but with You, no one or nothing can be against me!

Lord, thank You, for increasing my stature; to take me to the next level in my place of employment and in ministry. Touch me and my entire family so that we will also increase in peace, increase in vision, increase in our witness for Christ, increase in creativity, increase in health, increase in hearing Your voice, increase in godly friendships, increase in accountability, increase in self-control, increase in our discernment, increase in our ability to steward our resources well, increase in right decision-making, and increase in our communion with You.

Thank You, God, for Your favor and for Your anointing power. Thank You, for making people to be kind to me; to be conduits of opportunities and unexpected blessings. And in turn, for blessing me, that I may be a blessing to someone else. Thank You for also turning around situations that have caused me frustration.

Set in motion my faith as I obey your instructions. As I walk by faith, I do so with an expectation that my prayers are being answered. Help me to step into the right place, moving anything or anyone that stands in the way of me obtaining everything You have in store for me. Remove all barriers that could prevent me from hearing Your voice. Reveal to me any sinful ways that could block me from receiving the better portion from You, Lord. Lead me to repentance when need be; I want no prayer to go unheard or unanswered due to any sin of omission or commission. Lead me through the power of Your

Holy Spirit to humble myself, to lean not on my own understanding but to lean totally on You, Lord.

Thank You, for calling me an heir, a royal priesthood, and the redeemed of the Lord. Thank You, for making me the righteous through the work of Christ on Calvary. Thank You, for moving stones out of my way that would cause me to stumble. Thank You, for the medicine of Your Word that I daily take for complete healing and wholeness in my body, mind, and soul.

Lord, even when You don't reveal all the details to me about what You are doing, I will trust that You are working all things out for my good according to Your purpose for my life. I love You, and I plead the blood of Jesus Christ over every area assigned to my hands and every petition requesting Your intervention. I give Your name the praise, the glory,

and the honor and ask it all in the matchless name of my Risen Savior, Jesus Christ. Amen.

DECLARATION

I am increasing in wisdom, stature, and favor.

Please read Proverbs 1:7 and James 1:5. What do each of them say about wisdom? What areas in your life do you need to increase in the wisdom of God?

“Wisdom is not a product of schooling but of the lifelong attempt to acquire it.”
– Albert Einstein

DAY 16

GIVE ME PEACE

Be anxious for nothing, but in everything by prayer and supplication, with thanksgiving, let your requests be made known to God; and the peace of God, which surpasses all understanding, will guard your hearts and minds through Christ Jesus.
– Philippians 4:6-7

Gracious and Eternal God, I come before Your throne of grace in the name of my risen Savior, Jesus Christ. Lord, I praise You, and thank You, for the reminder that I have access to You regardless of the time of day or night. As I prepare to rest my body from a long day's work, I do so with the assurance that You are working all things out for my good.

Lord, through the power of Your Holy Spirit, I praise You for divine, supernatural peace; that peace that will help me to stand after I have done all I know to

do. Even in the midst of facing different battles all at the same time – relationship challenges, financial woes, juggling multiple projects, and increasing medical bills – I surrender it all to You, in exchange for Your peace. I can do so, knowing none of these battles are mine to fight; they all belong to You, Lord! You are my Defender, Provider, Sustainer, Strong-tower, and my Help, in time of trouble.

Like Jesus, help me to walk in that peace that positions me to fulfill the purpose in which I was born.

Peace that replaces the feelings of fear, anxiety, and worry.

Peace that testifies to the change that has taken place in my life.

Peace that shifts the course of my life to new dimensions.

Peace that strengthens and fortifies my faith.

Peace that leads to the fulfillment of my destiny.

Peace that breaks down self-imposed limitations and barriers.
Peace that endures when the bills are piling up, as the money is drying up.
Peace that Jesus spoke about during the storm when He said, "Peace, be still" (Mark 4:39).
I want that peace, that He spoke about when He declared, "Peace I leave with you, my peace I give unto you: not as the world gives, give I to you. Let not your heart be troubled, neither let it be afraid" (John 14:27).

Thank You, Lord, for unspeakable peace! I ask it all in the name of the One, who secures my peace, Jesus the Christ. Amen.

DECLARATION
I walk in peace.

Why is it so important for you to have peace abide in your heart? Is there a scripture that supports your feelings? If so, write it down and pen a prayer to God about your need for peace.

"If we have no peace, it is because we have forgotten that we belong to each other."
– Mother Teresa

DAY 17

PREGNANT WITH POSSIBILITY

"I am the Lord's servant," Mary answered. "May your word to me be fulfilled." Then the angel left her.
– Luke 1:38 (NIV)

Heavenly Father, it is with great joy and trepidation that I admit that I have been carrying around a promise. I confess to You, Father, often the fear of the unknown has kept me in denial of the symptoms and signs of the potential I have to birth something wonderful for Your Kingdom.

I admit that sometimes I feel like I am just going through the motions; I'm functioning but not at my best level. I'm serving but not with all I have to give. There are days that I operate from a place of great faith, I declare, "I believe all things are possible with

God!" And then there are those other days that I'm afraid of the *what if's* of life.

> *What if* I try and it does not work or I fail?
>
> *What if* I share my dream and it does not come to pass?
>
> *What if* I give my all, but my all is not good enough?
>
> *What if* I give away my love, but it is not reciprocated?
>
> *What if* I speak what You have revealed to me and no one believes me?
>
> *What if* I share the vision and something happens to kill it?

Lord, it appears that the *what if's* have been slowly draining me of my dreams and aspirations.

On many occasions I have *felt stuck*; like I'm on the sidelines watching others pursue their dreams. I've also *felt separated*, like an outcast not fitting into the preconceived boxes others have designed for my

containment. And then there are times I have *felt suffering*, many times in silence.

I am supposed to be strong; a mighty woman of God, a prayer warrior, one who stands in the gap for others. But on this particular night, I admit that I need someone to serve as an intercessor for me. I need angels to war on my behalf. I need the power of Your Spirit to encourage my heart.

In my spirit, I know that I am a *survivor*.

> I know You love me without conditions.
>
> I know You have brought me through many seen and unseen dangers.
>
> I know You have kept me when I didn't know I needed keeping.
>
> I know You have been my strength when I was weak.
>
> I know You are my peace in the midst of prevailing storms.

I know I am a royal priesthood, a chosen generation, and the redeemed of the Lord.

I know I am Your beloved daughter, the apple of Your eye.

I know the blood of Jesus Christ covers me.

I know that no weapon formed against me shall prosper.

I know that angels are encamped around me warring on my behalf.

And I know that I already have the victory in Jesus, that's why I'm still standing!

But sometimes, I feel tired.

Tired of being in pain.

Tired of feeling invisible.

Tired of feeling like I'm talking, but no one is listening.

Tired of dealing with people who lack vision.

Tired of people who say one thing but do another.

Tired of my contribution being minimized.

Tired of mediocrity and status quo thinking.

I am tired of ideas being stifled, dreams feeling deferred, and my creativity limited by lack of resources.

There is a fire burning inside of me and I desire for it to be released; to make a significant impact in this world! I want to produce something meaningful for the sake of the Kingdom!

I want to inspire some woman or man to live on purpose! I want to birth something that will live on long after I'm gone from this earth! I want to fulfill my purpose for living!

I need to speak!

I need to write!

I need to pray!

I need to exhort!

I need to lay hands!

I need to live my life with options!

God, I am a woman in transition! I just need Your touch through this process to bring forth possibility!

Help me to PUSH past the pain!

Help me to PUSH past the fear!

Help me to PUSH until my potential is realized!

God, I am calling on You, like a *travailing* woman who wants to produce something great for the Kingdom of God! In the wonderful name of Jesus, I pray. Amen.

[Several years ago, I attended the Woman Thou Art Loosed Conference in Dallas, Texas. Rev. Jasmin Sculark preached a sermon, "I Didn't Know I Was Pregnant" that resonated with me in such a profound way. When I left that arena, I wasted no time getting to my hotel room to commune with God in prayer. As I cried out to the Lord with tears streaming down my face, I felt the nudge of the Holy Spirit to pen this prayer. I am grateful to God for using Rev. "Jazz" to remind me that He wants to birth something amazing through me.]

DECLARATION

I am pregnant with possibility.

Stop allowing the "what if's" of life to drain you of your dreams and aspirations. Without apology or fear, ask God to use you to birth something great for His sake. Write it down. Include the necessary steps you must make to be successful. Submit it to God in prayer.

"Great minds discuss ideas,
average minds discuss events,
small minds discuss people."
– Eleanor Roosevelt

DAY 18

MY HEART'S DESIRE

May He grant you according to your heart's desire,
and fulfill all your purpose.
– Psalm 20:4

I woke up this morning excited about what the day may bring! Thank You, God, for the benefits package that comes along with serving You – the benefits of having You, as a Promise-keeper, Miracle-Worker, Storm Calmer, Way-maker, Refuge, Shelter, Protector, Provider, Redeemer, Sanctifier, Shelter, Healer, and Deliverer.

Lord, God, thank You, for the power of Your Word, for it transcends time; it remains relevant even today because You are the same yesterday, today, and forevermore.

Lord, God, I discern that You have more for me to do. As I embrace my purpose, it is my desire to serve You well.

You know the desires of my heart, Lord!

> Teach me patience, as I wait on You.
> Reveal to me Your will, as I walk in obedience.
> Show me how to rest in You, so I can stop worrying about tomorrow.
> Use me as an instrument of Your praise; a living epistle, who is unashamed of Your Gospel.

You know exactly what I need, Lord!

> Give me fresh revelation!
> Equip me for the work of ministry!

Impart wisdom, knowledge, and understanding so that I will make wise decisions!

Send the fire of Your Holy Spirit, to ignite me with power to fulfill my purpose!

Encamp angels around me, to ensure my safety for the journey!

Wake up what is sleeping in me, Lord!

Unlock Your favor!

Position me for supernatural increase!

Expose me to new ideas and strategies!

Give me the courage to do the impossible!

Prepare me for opened doors of opportunity!

Build me up to receive the gifts You, have designed specifically for me!

I cannot thank You enough for all that You do for me. I expect with great anticipation all the blessings You want to send my way. It is with honor, glory, and praise that I submit this prayer to You.

In the name of Jesus, I count it all done. Amen.

DECLARATION
God has a purpose for my life.

What is the desire of your heart? Does it align up with the Word of God? Find passages of Scripture to confirm that your heart's desire matches the heart of God.

God see's you and He knows the desire of your heart. Be thankful that You can count on Him to bring to fruition your hopes, dreams, and aspirations. Keep expecting God to show up in supernatural ways.

DAY 19

GOD IS MY SOURCE

And my God shall supply all your needs according to His riches in glory by Christ Jesus.
– Philippians 4:19

Heavenly Father, Heavenly Dove, I come before Your throne of grace once again with thanksgiving in my heart for being such a good God to me.

Thank You, God, for being my daily Source of wonderful benefits according to Psalm 68:19, "Blessed be the Lord, who daily loads us with benefits, the God of our salvation."

Thank You, God, for the foundation of Your promise to be a sufficient and capable Provider according to Matthew 6:30, "Now if God so clothes the grass of

the field, which today is, and tomorrow is thrown into the oven, will He not much more clothe you, O you of little faith?"

Thank You, God, for healing my body and for being so generous with Your blessings. According to Psalm 103:2-5, I am told to, "Forget not all His benefits: Who forgives all your iniquities, Who heals all your diseases, Who redeems your life from destruction, Who beautifies and dignifies, Who crowns you with loving-kindness and tender mercies, Who satisfies your mouth with good things, so that your youth is renewed like the eagle's."

Thank You, God, for teaching me how to delight myself in You and for the promise of being my Source of blessing and wealth. According to Psalm 112:1, 3, I am admonished to, "Praise the LORD! Blessed is the man who fears the LORD, who delights greatly in His commandments. Wealth and

riches will be in his house, and his righteousness endures forever."

Thanks You, God, for Your character and for Your sustaining grace towards me; for allowing me to prosper mightily. I am grateful for the words found in James 1:17, "Every good gift and every perfect gift is from above, and comes down from the Father of lights, with whom there is no variation or shadow of turning."

Thank You, Lord, for promising to leave no man or woman unrewarded because You are not a fraudulent God; You are trustworthy and truthful to keep Your Word. Thank You, for giving me favor with my employer, co-workers, colleagues, neighbors, and people I have yet to meet. Thank You, for the goodness, kindness, and encouragement of others along my journey. According to Lamentations 3:22-23, "Through the LORD's mercies we are not

consumed, because His compassions fail not. They are new every morning; Great is Your faithfulness."

Thank You, Lord, for our time together this morning. As I go about this day, I hope to bring glory and honor to Your Holy name. In the name of Jesus, I pray. Amen.

DECLARATION
God is my Source.

We live in a world that encourages self-sufficiency and self-reliance. Is there an area of your life that you need to fully trust God? To make Him your "Source"?

Once you have identified the areas you need to trust God with, make it a daily habit to surrender your tendency to do handle things your way and submit to God's way.

DAY 20

A PRAYER FOR MY SISTERS

For if you remain completely silent at this time, relief and deliverance will arise for the Jews from another place, but you and your father's house will perish. Yet who knows whether you have come to the kingdom for such a time as this?
– Esther 4:14 (NKJV)

Gracious and Eternal God, with adoration on my lips I come before Your throne of grace to say thank You for my sisters. I am so grateful for the mighty women You have put in my life. In this room are strong, courageous, beautiful, and gifted women. Women committed to serving as change agents for things yet to come. God, we are so very grateful for all that You have done for us over the years, and You have been faithful in keeping Your promises to us.

You have protected us from seen and unseen dangers.

You have opened doors of opportunity for us that were once closed.

You have healed our bodies when doctors told us there was no cure.

You have listened to our lament during troubling times.

You have calmed our soul in the midst of storms.

You have made our enemies our footstool.

You have loved us when others left us.

You have made provisions appear when we were fresh out of options.

You have honored us to be helpers to our mates, parents, and children.

You have orchestrated divine meetings with people who have become life-long friends.

You have brought peace when uncertainty overwhelmed us.

You have strengthened our faith when circumstances suggested that we walk in fear.

You have wiped away tears of disappointment and replaced them with tears of joy.

You have given us new perspectives when things did not go our way.

You have blessed us with tools for survival, in a sometimes cruel world.

You have brought people into our lives as teachers, mentors, adopted parents, advisors, counselors, coaches, play siblings, aunties, and sister girlfriends.

You have placed a love in our hearts to serve Your people.

You have expanded our capacity to hope, to dream, and to envision a better tomorrow.

Oh God, Thank You, for being so good to us! It is our joy to partner with You in service.

In the name of the most excellent Servant and Your greatest expression of love, Jesus Christ, we pray. Amen.

[This prayer was delivered at the Alpha Kappa Alpha Sorority, Incorporated, 2014 Metropolitan Founders' Day Celebration – "Celebrating Our Enduring Sisterhood and Remembering Our Legacy of Timeless Service"]

DECLARATION

I am my Sister's keeper.

I declare the blessings of the Lord over my Sister today. Write down the names of women whom God has used to bless your life over the years. How have they changed the course of your life? You may even want to write a personal note of gratitude to them.

I encourage you to nurture your relationships with other women. As I get older, I better appreciate the connection I have with my female friends – there is strength in sisterhood.

DAY 21

JESUS CAN HANDLE IT!

Surely He has borne our griefs, and carried our sorrows; yet we esteemed Him stricken, smitten by God, and afflicted. But He was wounded for our transgressions, He was bruised for our iniquities; the chastisement for our peace was upon Him, and by His stripes we are healed.
– Isaiah 53:4-5

Heavenly Father, I woke up this morning with my mind stayed on Jesus! You know that I have been praying for the right people, with the right skills and gifts, with the right resources, to assist me in several work-related ventures, the main one being the production and publication of the church magazine. So when a beloved member of the church expressed a willingness to financially support the printing of the magazine (sounds like an underwriter to me), I could not contain my joy!

I am so grateful for her generosity, but I am even more grateful for the words that came out of her mouth when I explained the cost associated with printing the magazines. She simply replied, "I can handle it!"

It's as if something leaped within my belly when I heard those four words, "I can handle it" roll off of her tongue; they have been running through my mind all night. Reflections about Jesus, His ministry, and His sacrificial love kept me up. I shudder at the thought of the Cross Jesus endured to handle what I was unqualified and ill-equipped to handle. He shouldered unnecessary baggage, taking on every sickness and disease so that I could walk in wholeness and fullness of joy! Lord, I feel a sermon coming over me! Jesus is saying, ***"I Can Handle It!"***

Jesus can handle whatever life brings my way!

That heartache, Jesus can handle it!

That disappointment, Jesus can handle it!

That sickness, Jesus can handle it!

That depression, Jesus can handle it!

That prodigal child, Jesus can handle it!

That loveless marriage, Jesus can handle it!

That jobless situation, Jesus can handle it!

That lack of confidence, Jesus can handle it!

That miscarriage, Jesus can handle it!

That lonely night, Jesus can handle it!

That raging storm, Jesus can handle it!

That mortgage, Jesus can handle it!

That death, Jesus can handle it!

That aging parent, Jesus can handle it!

That violation, Jesus can handle it!

That childhood trauma, Jesus can handle it!

That bad decision, Jesus can handle it!

The hurt you caused, Jesus can handle it!

The pain you inflicted, Jesus can handle it!

The sin you are entangled in, Jesus, can handle it!

The lie!

The fear!

The debt!

The violation!

JESUS can handle it!

JESUS can handle it!

JESUS can handle it!

Hallelujah!

He is worthy of the praise!

Thank You, God, for reminding me that there is absolutely nothing too hard for Jesus to handle! I ask it all in His mighty name. Amen.

DECLARATION
Jesus can handle it!

What must you entrust to Jesus today?

"When ends don't meet, even when they are too apart to even speak, what are you willing to trust God for?"

– Bishop Vashti McKenzie

DAY 22

YOU BETTER RECOGNIZE!

Surely goodness and mercy shall follow me all the days of my life; and I will dwell in the house of the LORD forever.
– Psalm 23:6

Good Morning God. I come before Your throne of grace with a spirit of thanksgiving in my heart and praise and adoration on my lips. You, are a wonderful, awesome, and loving God. I count it a joy and privilege to come into Your presence, expecting and anticipating You to speak to me this morning.

You deserve the highest praise and I shout Hallelujah in Your honor! I submit to the Lordship of Jesus Christ, as the Alpha and Omega of my life! I give

You, all the praise, glory, and honor for this is the day You have made, I will rejoice and be glad in it. Father God, You, are good and so worthy of worship and praise, for Your mercy endures forever!

Lord, over the next ten days, it is my intention to press into Your presence with the hope that You will oblige me accordingly, by pressing back. I am committing the first three hours of my waking day to spending time in Your presence – basking in Your glory, communing with You, worshipping You in Spirit and in truth, singing praises unto Your name, spending time reading Your Word, discerning Your will for my life, and journaling promptings of Your Spirit. Send Your revelation, Lord, and give me a yielded spirit to obey with swiftness. I deem this time sacred as I seek Your instructions and directives.

Lord, I consecrate this time to You and I surrender any and all things that could serve as a hindrance to discerning Your voice – every burden, care, worry, doubt, fear, and any anxious thoughts. I do so with full assurance that You can handle every single situation, circumstance, or problem; I know that I am in good hands because You have proven Yourself over and over again to be trustworthy, honesty, and dependable.

Therefore, I trust You, Lord, with every detail of my life and I thank You for the sufficiency of Your provisions of grace, mercy, forgiveness, peace, joy, and unconditional love.

Search my heart, O Lord. Cleanse me now, so that nothing will get in the way of me receiving from You. Forgive me for the times that I have fallen short of Your glory. Forgive me for those occasions that I have sinned against You, in how I treated my sister

and brother. Have mercy upon me, O Lord, for I am the one standing in need of prayer!

Thank You, Lord!
Thank You, for the gift of forgiveness and restoration!
Thank You, for seeing me through the lens of Jesus!
Thank You, for the shed blood of Jesus!
Thank You, for the power of Your Holy Spirit!
Thank You, for redeeming my soul!
Thank You, for deliverance!
Thank You, for sanctification!
Thank You, for healing!
Thank You, for breaking every chain of bondage devised for my destruction.
Thank You, for Your will and purpose is being fulfilled in my life.

Speak Lord!

I am listening!
My heart is pliable!
My mind is receptive!
My will is surrendered!
I have an ear to hear!
I need Your guidance and instruction!
Please, speak Lord!

Send the rain!

Rain Your blessings of prosperity!
Rain Your blessings of abundance!
Rain Your blessings of favor!
Rain Your blessings of wisdom!
Rain Your blessings of discernment!
Rain Your blessings of healing!
Rain Your blessings of anointing power!

I give You, all the praise, glory, and honor. In the name of, Jesus. Amen.

DECLARATION

I commit to spending time with God every day.

Submit to the Lordship of Jesus today. Surrender to His will for Your life. On the lines below, write down areas that you struggle giving Him complete control.

"God doesn't want something from you. He wants something for you. Your value is not in what you do (as if you could ever do enough) but in who you are (as if you could ever be more loved and accepted by Him than you already are)."

– Priscilla Shirer

DAY 23

GOD IS MY EVERYTHING

. . . one God and Father of all, who is above all, and through all, and in you all.
– Ephesians 4:6

My God, You, are wonderful, marvelous, and glorious!

You are the Alpha and the Omega, the beginning and the end.

You are Omnipotent, all powerful and there is nothing too hard for You to handle.

You are Omniscient, all knowing, all wise, and sovereign; You, even know my thoughts.

You are Omnipresent; You are everywhere all at the same time! Your existence is indescribable.

You are Immutable, the God who never changes;

You are the same yesterday, today, and forevermore!
My God, You, are my peace in the midst of a storm; my shelter when I need covering; my help in time of trouble; and my light in the midst of darkness.
My God, You, are bread when I'm hungry; and my thirst quencher when I'm in need of refreshing.
My God, You, are the Great "I AM".
Whatever I stand in need of, I can trust You to BE.
You are:

My Good Shepherd;
My Banner;
My Refuge;
My Fortress;
My Deliverer;
My Sanctifier;
My Provider;
My Healer;
My Physician;
My Lawyer;
My Teacher,
My Accountant;
My Sustainer;
My Defender;

My Protector;
My Strength;
My Redeemer;
My Savior;
and My Lord!

Thank You, God, for being all things to me as I look to You to meet my needs! In Jesus' name, I pray. Amen.

DECLARATION
God is my everything!

How has God, demonstrated to you that He is the Great “I AM” in your life?

"When we don't know, we must be satisfied to know the One Who knows. If we are going to walk with Him and enjoy His blessings, we must learn to let God, be God."
– Joyce Meyer

DAY 24

HEALING IS MINE FOR THE ASKING

Death and life are in the power of the tongue, and those who love it will eat its fruit.
– Proverbs 18:21

Good Morning, Heavenly Father! I have so much to be thankful for as it pertains to my health.

I praise You, this morning for the start of another day!

I praise You, for last night's restful sleep!

I praise You, for my portion of health and strength!

I praise You, for Your keeping power!

I praise You, for the blood of Jesus, and for the privilege to call on Your name!

I praise You, for what Christ has already done for me; He has purchased my healing!

I praise You, for being an approachable God; as I draw near to You, the favor is returned!
I praise You, for the power of Your Holy Spirit, who comforts, directs, and gives me peace!
I praise You, for touching me with Your finger of love this morning!
Lord, I glorify and bless Your Holy name!

Thank You, Father, that healing is for my entire family according to Genesis 20:17.

Thank You, Father, that You are the author of good health (Genesis 43:28).

Thank You, Father, for counter-attacking the enemy's attack of affliction according to Genesis 50:20, "… as for you, you meant evil against me; but God meant it for good, in order to bring it about as it is this day, to save many people alive."

Thank You, Father, for being God the Lord who heals me (Exodus 15:26).

Thank You, Father, for healing my body of every disease (Leviticus 13:18).

Thank You, Father, for cleansing and purifying me from every evidence of sickness (Leviticus 13:37).

Thank You, Father, for healing me according to Numbers 12:13, "Moses cried out to the LORD, saying, 'Please heal her, O God I pray.'"

Thank You, Father, for delivering me and setting me free from bondage and affliction according to Numbers 15:41, "I am the LORD your God, who brought you out of the land of Egypt, to be your God: I am the LORD your God."

Thank You, Father, that as I put my trust in You and obey Your Word I am healed according to Deuteronomy 28:1-2.

Thank You, Father, that You alone are the source of my healing according to Deuteronomy 32:29, "Now see that I, even I, am He, and there is no God beside Me…"

Thank You, Father, for healing "the brokenhearted and for binding up their wounds" according to Psalm 147:3.

Thank You, Father, for Jesus has the power to heal according to Matthew 9:35, "Jesus went through all the towns and villages, teaching in their synagogues, proclaiming the good news of the kingdom and healing every disease and sickness."

Thank You, Father, for strengthening my faith as I trust You to heal my body according to Mark 5:34, "He said to her, 'Daughter, your faith has healed you. Go in peace and be freed from your suffering.'"

Thank You, Father, for I have no reason to be afraid; "Peace I leave you; My peace I give you. I do not give to you as the world gives. Do not let your hearts be troubled and do not be afraid" (John 14:27).

Thank You, Father, for always being in control. I will not fear because You have told me in Philippians 4:6, "Do not be anxious about anything, by prayer and petition, with thanksgiving, present your requests to God."

Thank You, Father, for meeting my every need as declared in Philippians 4:19, "And my God will meet all your needs according to the riches of His glory in Christ Jesus."

Thank You, Father, for the promises of Your Word found in James 5:14-15, "Is anyone among you sick? Let them call the elders of the church to pray over them and anoint them with oil in the name of the Lord. And the prayer offered in faith will make the sick person well; the Lord will raise them up. If they have sinned, they will be forgiven."

Thank You, Father, for Jesus; according to 1 Peter 2:24, "Who Himself bore our sins in His own body on the tree, that we, having died to sins, might live for righteousness – by whose stripes you were healed."

I ask for these and all needful blessings, in the mighty name of Jesus, my Strength, my Redeemer, and my Healer. Amen.

DECLARATION

I am healed by the stripes of Jesus.

Do you need healing in your body? Is your mind in need of renewing? Begin to meditate on the Word of God as you submit every ache, pain, sickness, and disease into His capable hands. Write a prayer to God to heal whatever ails you on the lines below.

"Take care of your body. It's the only place you have to live."
– Jim Rohn

DAY 25

GOD IS FAITHFUL

Let us hold fast the confession of our hope without wavering, for He who promised is faithful.
– Hebrews 10:23

Heavenly Father, Heavenly Dove, how wonderful to have the honor of spending time in Your presence one more time! To bask in Your glory is my greatest reward! Thank You for the privilege of having Your Word, for Your Word allows me to daily renew my mind by aligning my thoughts and words with it.

Father, I ask You to open my eyes to see with Holy Ghost vision; open up my ears to hear Your voice with clarity and understanding; prick my heart that it might be found pliable and receptive to Your teachings. Give me Holy Ghost revelation so that I will know how to bring to fruition the vision You have for my family, my home, my finances, my job, and my ministry.

Father, I know that the promises You speak about in the Bible are for me too. I come into agreement with what You have already said in Your Word about who I am, and I fill the atmosphere with Your promises.

I am reminded of what happened when Ezekiel took You at Your Word and spoke life into a dead situation; dead bones lived again! Please help me to feed my faith when times are challenging, when uncertainty arises, or when I simply don't know what to do next, for "Faith comes by hearing and hearing by the Word of God" (Romans 10:17).

Lord, according to Proverbs 18:21, "The power of life and death is in my tongue." Help me to only speak life into my situations and circumstances. As

I continue to ask, seek, and knock please raise high my antenna of discernment to know what and how to pray. Give me the articulation of my lips, and Holy Ghost insight to be effective as I fervently pray.

In the matchless name of Jesus, I charge the atmosphere with my praise and worship. I bless Your name! I glorify You, Lord! I magnify You, God! There is none like You in heaven or in earth! I adore You! I love You! I bless Your Holy name!

Thank You, Lord, for opening divine gateways of access, information, and insight.
Thank You, Lord, for prosperity, abundance, and for generational blessings.
Thank You, Lord, for deliverance from ungodly people and situations.
Thank You, Lord, for teaching me how to wisely conduct my affairs.

Thank You, Lord, for discernment of the seasons and times.
Thank You, Lord, for understanding to handle conflict in a godly manner.
Thank You, Lord, for giving me strategies to meet deadlines and assignments.
Thank You, Lord, for allowing only those with divine purpose to be drawn to me.
Thank You, Lord, for surrounding me with men and women who serve as wise counsel.
Thank You, Lord, for the victory through Jesus Christ!

In the majestic and mighty name of Jesus, I pray. Amen.

DECLARATION

God is faithful.

Words are containers; they have power and the ability to shape your life. What words do you frequently use? Do they build up or tear down others? What words do you use to describe yourself? Do your words bring glory and honor to God?

"The older you get the more faith you should have because you've experienced more of God's faithfulness. And it is God's faithfulness that increases our faith and enlarges our dreams."
– Mark Batterson

DAY 26

PURPOSE IN MY PAIN

... those who followed were shouting, "Hosanna! Blessed is the one who comes in the name of the Lord!"
– Mark 11:9

Father, God, I honor Your name for You, alone are worthy! I lift my voice to sing Your praises, for You, are wonderful! I rejoice in knowing that there is purpose in my pain!

Today is Palm Sunday and churches throughout the globe commemorate the triumphal entry of Jesus into Jerusalem riding on a donkey. Preachers mounted pulpits, retelling an old story with the hopes of saying something relevant and practical for the problems of today. Choirs sang various renditions of "Hosanna" reminding us that, "Blessed is the one who comes in

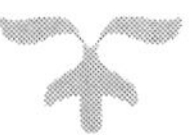

the name of the Lord" as liturgical dancers expressed their adoration through movement of their hands and feet. Ushers distributed palms as churchgoers exited houses of worship in preparation of Holy Week, reminding us that Friday is coming.

To think, many of the same people who were shouting, "Hosanna!" in celebration of what Jesus had done for them were now shouting, "Crucify Him!" just days later. To think, He would also experience the pain of betrayal and denial from the very men He called disciples; but Jesus knew there was purpose in His pain. There could be no crown without the cross.

There was purpose in His pain. His love for humanity took into consideration our filthiness. He looked past our sinfulness and saw our need for a Savior; His love for me was greater than my sin! God, You, released into the earth, Your greatest

expression of love. Jesus took a leave of absence from the heavenly realm, to take up the mantle of a Suffering Servant in the earth; for thirty-three years to be exact.

There was purpose in His pain. He went about tending to the business of His Father – confronting corruption within the temple; meeting the needs of the widows, the little children, the sick, the diseased, the demon-possessed, the naked, the hungry, the broken, the helpless, the left out, the prodigal, and the sinner. "The Son of Man did not come to be served. He came to serve others and to give His life as a ransom for many people" (Mark 10:45).

He humbled Himself as a Servant leader, washing the feet of His disciples. He took a towel and a basin to teach about leadership – what a peculiar teaching technique. No assignment was too menial when done with great love.

Father, as an image-bearer of my Lord and Savior, I too want to find purpose in my pain. Perhaps, the challenges I have faced are just building blocks to greater character and integrity. The deferred dream is not a denial but purely an opportunity to practice patience and perseverance. The disappointments are simply occasions to strengthen my backbone as I humbly submit to Your Lordship.

There is purpose in my pain. The losses have taught me to trust in Your sovereignty; Your ways and thoughts are so very different and superior to mine. The business endeavor that failed, the relationship dynamics that changed, the financial crisis that occurred, the unexpected health challenge – none of it is wasted.

There is purpose in my pain. To fortify my faith, to test my commitment, to solidify my trust in Your timing. "For we walk by faith, not by sight" (2

Corinthians 5:7). This journey is indeed a faith walk, and I am trusting You to see me through to the finish line.

There is purpose in my pain. To be better equipped to help someone else who is broken-hearted; to speak a word of encouragement, "This too shall pass." To comfort someone who just buried the love of their life, or to remind someone struggling to make ends meet, "God can turn it on a dime!" To serve the least of these; the marginalized, the forgotten, the castaway, and the impoverished.

Thank You, God, for the witness of Jesus; for His life exemplifies for me how I should handle pain, suffering, disappointment, and loss. "Don't' ever give up!" are the words that resonate in my mind. All of it has purpose. What the enemy meant for evil You, will use it for my good! All of it is working for my good! All of it! Hallelujah!

In the name of Jesus, I pray. Amen.

DECLARATION

There is purpose in my pain.

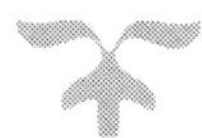

In looking back over your life, can you see how God used a hardship or difficult time to bring glory to His name? To strengthen you for life's journey?

“God has a purpose for your pain, a reason for your struggle, and a reward for your faithfulness. Don’t give up.”

– Author Unknown

DAY 27

AT THE FOOT OF THE CROSS

For Christ also suffered once for sins, the just for the unjust, that He might bring us to God, being put to death in the flesh but made alive by the Spirit.
– 1 Peter 3:18

Gracious and Eternal God, when I survey the wondrous work of the Cross my soul cries out Hallelujah! I come praying in the name of Jesus, grateful for the foot of the Cross.

At the foot of the Cross, I surrender every present feeling of insecurity, uncertainty, worry, doubt, and fear.

At the foot of the Cross, I place every memory that conjures up feelings of torment, affliction, abandonment, unworthiness, and condemnation.

At the foot of the Cross, I disavow every believed accusation, lie, and untruth spoken over my life.

At the foot of the Cross, I release every hurt, disappointment, and unfulfilled dream.

At the foot of the Cross, I leave every fiery dart of the enemy; roadblocks, stumbling stones, traps, tricks, and distractions created to take me off course.

At the foot of the Cross, I relinquish every generational curse and stronghold of not enough, lack, poverty, and debt.

At the foot of the Cross, I lay down every spirit of pride, bitterness, and resentment.

At the foot of the Cross, I submit every sickness, ailment, disease, and painful experience.

At the foot of the Cross, I entrust every member of my family, friends, co-workers, colleagues, neighbors, associates, and church family members.

Thank You, God, for the work of the Cross that secures my salvation, redemption, deliverance, healing, and provision.

Thank You, God, for covering me in the blood of Jesus, my suffering Savior, my crucified Healer, and my resurrected Redeemer.

I ask it all in the precious name of the One who endured the Cross for the sake of all humanity, the Nazarene carpenter from Galilee, Jesus the Christ! Amen.

DECLARATION

I place every concern at the foot of the Cross.

What do you need to place at the foot of the Cross today? Write it below and submit it to the Lord in prayer.

"It was something natural that *hurt* you, but you need something supernatural to *heal* you."
– Bishop Walter S. Thomas

DAY 28

GOD IS TRUSTWORTHY

My times are in Your hands . . .
– Psalm 31:15

Gracious and Eternal God, in the name of Jesus Christ, we humbly come before Your throne of grace with Holy Ghost boldness because we know You to be an all knowing, all wise, wonder working God, and we trust You with every detail of our lives!

We know You, to be a TRUSTWORTHY GOD! You are the same yesterday, today, and forevermore. You have an ear to hear the cries of Your children. You love us unconditionally. A God of another chance, You, look past our faults and see our need for a Healer, a Deliverer, a Provider, a Sanctifier, a Reconciler, a Redeemer, and a Savior.

We know You, to be a FAITHFUL GOD!
You meet us in our desert places. You come to see about us in the midst of our affliction. You wipe our tears away in moments of despair. You provide peace during our storms. You give us rest in times of weariness, strength when we are weak, restoration when we are broken, joy in our struggles, comfort for our sorrows, and sunshine after the rain.

We know You, to be a WAY-MAKING GOD!
You write our prescriptions when we are sick. You are our refuge in times of trouble. You are our Defender in the courtroom. You are our Caretaker to prodigal sons and daughters, our Source when our resources are depleted, and our mind regulator during stressful times. You are our GPS when we are lost,

and our hedge of protection from every scheme and attack of the enemy.

We know You, to be a PROMISE-KEEPING GOD!

You never leave us nor forsake us. You honor Your Word and You are no respecter of persons. We can call on You any time of the day or night and You will answer us. We are covered by the blood of Jesus, and filled with the power of Your Holy Spirit. You order our steps, anoint our heads with oil, and extend to us Your grace and Your mercy. You forgive our sins, and pour out abundant blessings upon our lives that those connected to us benefit from the overflow.

We know You, to be an AWESOME GOD!

We serve as witnesses and testify that You, are a praise-worthy God! A God deserving of our adoration and thanksgiving! A God to be magnified! A God to be exalted! A God that welcomes our

worship! A God that rejoices in getting glory out of our lives! When we think about Your goodness, and all that You have done for us, our souls cry out, Hallelujah!

We know You, to be an ON TIME GOD!

Father, we need to hear from You! Your ways and thoughts are so different than ours; that's why we run to You when we need an answer for our problem, a miracle for our mess, a solution for our situation, a directive for our dilemma, and an instruction for our circumstance. Father, we are asking, we are seeking, and we are knocking! Speak Lord, Your, children are listening! Your sons and daughters have need of You!

O, God, how excellent is Your name in all the earth!

We seal this prayer in the wonderful name of Jesus, our Strength and our Redeemer. Amen.

DECLARATION

My God is trustworthy.

What or whom are you putting your trust in? Is it in your friends, job, finances, education, or your abilities? Make a decision today to put your complete trust in God.

"Every woman has needs. But many of us are guilty of looking to other people to meet them – especially the men in our lives. We expect too much from *them* when our expectations should be in *God*."

– Stormie Omartian

DAY 29

AGREE WITH THE WORD OF GOD

But what does it say? "The word is near you, in your mouth and in your heart" (that is, the word of faith which we preach): that if you confess with your mouth the Lord Jesus and believe in your heart that God has raised Him from the dead, you will be saved."
– Romans 10:8-9

Gracious and Eternal God, thank You, for another day of life, health, and strength to agree with Your Word. We need reinforcement today as we strive to live for You and not this world. We continue to stand on the foundation of Your promises found in the Scriptures, speaking into the atmosphere what You say about us with grateful hearts:

We are joint heirs with Jesus! – Romans 8:17

We are justified by faith! – Romans 5:1

We are free from all condemnation! – Romans 8:1

We are crucified and made alive with Christ! – Galatians 2:20

We are the temple of the Holy Spirit! – 1 Corinthians 6:19

We are Your beloved children, the apples of Your eyes! – Psalm 17:8

We are saved by grace! – Ephesians 2:8

We are redeemed by the blood of the Lamb! – Ephesians 1:7

We are forgiven of all our sins! – 1 John 2:12

We are new creatures in Christ! – 2 Corinthians 5:17

We are part of Your royal priesthood! – 1 Peter 2:9

We are Your elect! – Titus 1:1

We are counted as members of a chosen generation! – 1 Peter 2:9

We are the salt of the earth! – Matthew 5:13

We are the light of the world! – Matthew 5:14

We are fearfully and wonderfully made in Your image! – Psalm 139:14

We are firmly rooted, built up, and established in the faith! – Colossians 2:7

We are the head and not the tail! – Deuteronomy 28:13a

We are first and not the last! – Matthew 20:16

We are above and not beneath! – Deuteronomy 26:13b

We are complete in Christ! – Colossians 2:10

We are disciples of Christ! – John 12:26

We are saints! – Romans 1:7

We are strong in the Lord! – Philippians 4:13

We are more than conquerors through Christ who strengthens us! – Romans 8:37

We are the righteousness of God! – 2 Corinthians 5:21

We are healed by the stripes of Jesus Christ! – 1 Peter 2:24

We are filled with the power of the Holy Spirit! – Romans 8:11

We are God's workmanship created in Christ Jesus! – Ephesians 2:10

We are protected by angels! – Psalm 91:11; Luke 4:10

We are transformed by the renewing of our minds! – Romans 12:2

We are saved! – Romans 10:9-10

We are delivered! – John 10:9-11

We are overtaken with blessings! – Deuteronomy 28:2

We are blessed with all spiritual blessings in heavenly places! – Ephesians 1:3

We are prosperous! – Joshua 1:8

Our steps are ordered by the Lord! – Psalm 37:23

We thank You, God, for all that we are through our Lord and Savior, Jesus Christ!

We are the redeemed of the Lord, and we say so! Amen.

DECLARATION

I choose to agree with the Word of God.

Spend some time reading the Word of God today.
Jot down the biblical truths found in His Word
about who you are in Him.

"Always go with the Word of God, because your circumstances will lie to you."
– Dr. Maurice Watson

DAY 30

BUT I'M STILL STANDING

... and, lo, I am with you always, even unto the end of the age.
– Matthew 28:20b

Ye are of God, little children, and have overcome them: because greater is He that is in you, than he that is in the world.
– John 4:4

Lord, when I consider where You have brought me from, and what You have brought me through, and You are not finished with me yet my soul cries out Hallelujah! In spite of everything I've gone through – the messes, the tests, the troubles, the trials, the situations, I'm still standing! You have been mighty good to me!

The devil tried to destroy me, but I'm still standing. Endured some lonely nights, but I'm still standing.

Gone through various storms, but I'm still standing.

Battled sickness, but I'm still standing.

Insufficient funds, but I'm still standing.

Felt the sting of betrayal, but I'm still standing.

Experienced disappointment, but I'm still standing.

Suffered great sorrow, but I'm still standing.

Tasted defeat, but I'm still standing.

Some dreams deferred, but I'm still standing.

Encountered tough times, but I'm still standing.

Contribution minimized, but I'm still standing.

Character attacked, but I'm still standing.

I've been lied on, overlooked, dismissed, and counted out, but I'm still standing!

Thank You, God, the setbacks were only temporary!

Hallelujah!

My victory is already won!

My hope is secured in Christ!

My salvation is paid in full!

My faith is fortified!

My character is built up!

My backbone is strong!

My head is lifted!

My heart is receptive!

My countenance is humbled!

My will is surrendered!

My discernment is on high alert!

My steps are ordered by the Lord!

I am blood washed and Spirit-filled!

I am appointed, anointed, and on assignment!

I am a daughter of the Most High God!

There is nothing too hard for my God to handle!

That's why I keep blessing Your Holy name!

Every chance I get I will bless Your Holy name!

You are worthy of the praise!

You are deserving of the glory and honor!

Lord, You, make all the difference!

You, are the reason why I'm still standing!

You, have been good to me!

You, have been better to me than I could ever be to myself!

You, looked passed my faults and saw all of my needs!

You, saw my need for a Healer, Deliverer, Redeemer, and Savior!

Hallelujah!

I am grateful!

Thank You, Lord!

In the marvelous name of Jesus, I pray. Amen.

DECLARATION

I declare that I will keep standing.

You too are still standing because of the goodness of the Lord! Write down a time when God saw you through a difficult time, a sticky situation, or an unbearable crisis.

God is never surprised by the challenges you face. So instead of yielding to the trials and troubles, look at them as opportunities to depend on Him.

DAY 31

KEEP ON PRAYING

Rejoice always, pray continually, give thanks in all circumstances; for this is God's will for you in Christ Jesus.
– 1 Thessalonians 5:16 (NIV)

Merciful Father, I come before Your throne of grace with thanksgiving in my heart. I magnify Your Holy name for You alone are worthy of my praise and adoration! It is so wonderful to commune with You, on this new day full of possibility and promise.

Lord, I praise You, because Your providence is at work in my life; nothing is by happenstance, chance, luck, or coincidence but You, alone are orchestrating the details of my life. That's why I keep on asking, and I keep on seeking, and I keep on knocking

because I trust that You, will keep on hearing my prayers.

So please give me mountain moving power in my mouth. Build up my faith like that of a child, and strengthen my character as You widen my capacity for more. I know my prayers matter to You Lord, so I will keep on praying:

Keep on praying for the blood of Jesus Christ to cover me.

Keep on praying for the power of Your Holy Spirit to lead me.

Keep on praying for angels to encamp around me.

Keep on praying for a closer walk with You.

Keep on praying for wisdom and guidance.

Keep on praying for grace and mercy.

Keep on praying for humility.

Keep on praying for meekness.

Keep on praying for long-suffering.

Keep on praying for forgiveness.

Keep on praying for a stronger and healthier marriage.

Keep on praying for generational blessings.

Keep on praying for the salvation of my loved ones.

Keep on praying for deliverance of those who are bound.

Keep on praying for the ability to create wealth for my family.

Keep on praying for peace in the earth.

Keep on praying for the naked to be clothed.

Keep on praying for the hungry to be fed.

Keep on praying for the homeless to find shelter.

Keep on praying for provision for the widows and orphans.

Keep on praying for broken families to be restored.

Keep on praying for prodigal sons and daughters to come back home.

Keep on praying for justice to roll down.

Keep on praying for the end to senseless killings.

Keep on praying for food and water in countries plagued with famine and drought.

Keep on praying for world leaders to walk in wisdom.

Keep on praying for politicians to be men and women of integrity.

Keep on praying for the unemployed to find work.

Keep on praying for the sick and afflicted to be made well.

Keep on praying for barren wombs to experience birthing pangs.

Keep on praying for the bereaved to be comforted.

Keep on praying for the caregiver to be refreshed.

Keep on praying for the castaway to be found.

Keep on praying for the weak to be made strong.

Keep on praying for the lonely to have companionship.

Keep on praying for broken-hearts to be mended.

Keep on praying for the stability of tormented minds.

Keep on praying for babies yet to be born.

Keep on praying for our children and youth.

Keep on praying for our senior citizens.

Keep on praying for our veterans.

Keep on praying for our military personnel.

Keep on praying for first responders – police officers, fire fighters, and emergency medical technicians.

Keep on praying for educators.

Keep on praying for medical professionals – doctors, nurses, and therapists.

Keep on praying for business owners.

Keep on praying for the church to be a House of prayer.

Keep on praying for preachers of the gospel.

Keep on praying for pastors of churches.

Keep on praying for televangelists.

Keep on praying for missionaries.

Keep on praying for deacons, trustees, and elders.

Keep on praying for ministry leaders.

Keep on praying for musicians and psalmists.
Keep on praying for the righteous to rule.
Keep on praying for holiness to prevail.
Keep on praying for our gifts to be stirred up and used.
Keep on praying for the transformation of our communities.
I will keep on praying for my Heavenly Father to hear the cries of His earthbound daughter!
I will keep on praying because You specialize in signs, wonders, and miracles!
I will keep on praying because You have proven to me that You can be trusted!
I will keep on praying because You have a plan and purpose for my life!
I will keep on praying because You are not finished with me yet!
I will keep on praying Lord, until my change comes!

Asking it all in the name of Jesus. Amen.

DECLARATION

I will keep on praying.

No matter the length of time, keep praying for the desires of your heart. Make a list of your prayer concerns and Keep Praying Until Something Happens! PUSH!

Keep on praying until something happens – PUSH!

"Faith is acting like it's so, even when it's not so, in order that it might be so, simply because God said so."
– Dr. Tony Evans

ABOUT THE AUTHOR

The Reverend Adriane Larau Blair Wise is Minister of Christian Spiritual Formation at the historic Metropolitan Baptist Church. She is responsible for all educational programming, spiritual and leadership development, as well as training of all teachers and instructors. In this capacity, she also serves as staff minister for the following ministries: P.U.S.H. Prayer Ministry, the Charles S. Whitted New Disciples Ministry, Sunday School, Mentor Program for Girls, Girl Scouts, Christian Discipleship Council, and the H. Beecher Hicks, Jr. Library Ministry. She also gives leadership for the Christian Discipleship Institute, also serving as an instructor. Rev. Wise is also the Minister of Licensure and Ordination, providing guidance, training, and mentorship for Associate Ministers as they prepare for the ordained ministry. Most recently she served as a Teaching Assistant at Wesley Theological Seminary for Preaching and Worship and as an Adjunct Professor at Prince Georges Community College.

Rev. Wise spent eight years at the District of Columbia Baptist Convention, holding several

positions during her tenure. Her most recent post was as the Principal Coordinator/Consultant for the Center for Ministerial Leadership, offering continuing education, ministerial leadership and development, pastoral care, and training programs for over 150 churches within the DC/Metropolitan area. Prior to this assignment, she served as the Director of Higher Education Ministries, overseeing campus ministry efforts for seven colleges/universities (Howard University, American University, Gallaudet University, Georgetown University, George Washington University, University of Maryland, and University of District of Columbia); while serving in this role she also served for eight years as the Baptist Chaplain at Howard University and for two years at American University. Reverend Wise also served at Mt. Gilead Baptist Church for seven years as the Assistant Minister for Discipleship Development and Membership Training and as the Administrative Assistant to the Senior Pastor.

Rev. Wise is a graduate of Wesley Theological Seminary earning a Master of Divinity degree with a concentration in Preaching and Worship. While a student, she served as President of the Association of Black Seminarians, a member of the Student Council, and the Baptist House of Studies. Upon graduation, she received the Community Service

Award. She also traveled to South Africa as a member of an immersion experience. Rev. Wise earned a Bachelor of Science degree in Business Administration and Management and a Certification in African-American Studies both from Stockton University in New Jersey.

Rev. Wise also has numerous affiliations and awards to her recognition. She holds membership in the American Baptist Churches, USA; District of Columbia Baptist Convention, Leadership Greater Washington, National Association for the Advancement of Colored People (NAACP), and National Association of Professional Women (NAPW).

She is also a Life Member of Alpha Kappa Alpha Sorority, Inc., celebrating 31 years of active service this year. Currently, she serves as Chaplain for Rho Mu Omega Chapter. She has also served on numerous committees including the Health Committee (Chairman) and the Jazz Brunch Auction (Vice-Chairman). She is the recipient of the 2016 Top Fundraiser of the Year Award, 2014 Outstanding Silver Star Award, 2014 Most Sisterly Soror Award, and 1998 Outstanding Community Service Award. In addition, she was appointed by the International President to serve on the International Day of Prayer Committee. She was

also appointed by the North Atlantic Regional Director as the Regional Chaplain and Prayer Team Chairman. Prior to this office, she served as Co-Chairman of the Prayer Team. In 2017 she worked as the Chairman for the North Atlantic Regional Conference Ecumenical Service, a position she also held in 2010. She has also served as the guest preacher for the Ecumenical Service.

Rev. Wise is the Founder and President of Wise Practices, LLC. She has been in ministry for over twenty-five years and is a sought out speaker, teacher, prayer intercessor, facilitator, mentor, and life coach. Rev. Wise is from Willingboro, New Jersey and is the proud wife of Reverend Ryan A. Wise.

Made in the USA
Middletown, DE
29 May 2019